Russian Mirror
Three Plays by
Russian Women

translated and edited by
Melissa T. Smith
Youngstown State University, Ohio, USA

harwood academic publishers

Australia • Canada • China • France • Germany • India
Japan • Luxembourg • Malaysia • The Netherland
Russia • Singapore • Switzerland

Amsteldijk 166
1st Floor
1079 LH Amsterdam
The Netherlands

Applications for licences to perform *On the Road to Ourselves* should be addressed to Maria Arbatova, Ussatchova Street 25, apt. 6, Moscow 119046, Russia.

Applications for licences to perform *Behind the Mirror* should be addressed to Elena Gremina, Krasnoarmeyskaia Street 25, apt. 9, Moscow 125319, Russia.

Applications for licences to perform *Russian Dream* should be addressed to Olga Mikhailova, Trekhprudnyi pereulok 11/13, apt. 3, Moscow 103001, Russia.

British Library Cataloguing in Publication Data

Russian mirror: three plays by Russian women. – (Russian
   theatre archive; v. 14)
   1. Catherine, II, Empress of Russia, 1729–1796 – Drama
   2. Russian drama – 20th century – Translations into English
   3. Russia – History – Drama   4. Soviet Union – Emigration and
   immigration – Drama   5. Soviet Union – Social conditions –
   1970–1991 – Drama
   I. Smith, Melissa T.   II. Arbatova, Maria. On the road to
   ourselves   III. Grimina, Elena. Behind the mirror
   IV. Mikhailova, Olga. Russian dream
   891.7'25

ISBN 90-5755-025-3   1001350651
            9057550245   T

*For all the Russians and Americans,
women and men, who saw this project
through to its conclusion*

CONTENTS

INTRODUCTION TO THE SERIES

The Russian Theatre Archive makes available in English the best avant-garde plays from the pre-Revolutionary period to the present day. It features monographs on major playwrights and theatre directors, introductions to previously unknown works, and studies of the main artistic groups and periods.

Plays are presented in performing edition translations, including (where appropriate) musical scores, and instructions for music and dance. Whenever possible the translated texts will be accompanied by videotapes of performances of plays in the original language.

INTRODUCTION

The three playwrights presented together in this volume, Maria Arbatova (*On the Road to Ourselves*), Elena Gremina (*Behind the Mirror*), and Olga Mikhailova (*Russian Dream*) reflect an image of Russia that is both new and old. The new post-Soviet era, though characterized by a freer intellectual climate, is one fraught with new difficulties for the theater. With the decline of state subsidies, the economic realities of the box-office, long familiar to Western writers, hit writers and artists especially hard. The road to critical recognition for the writers here has not been easy: while continually shining at national festivals for young playwrights, their works have had scant opportunities on the professional stage. At the same time, I believe that these plays contain many elements which should appeal to Western directors and audiences: well-drawn characters, engaging plots, lively wit. Central to the three plays selected for this volume is a complex interaction of Russian and Western value systems, a theme that becomes more and more relevant for Russian audiences with each passing season, and, I think, no less relevant for Europeans and Americans.

Freed from dictates about "what" to write, whether formally imposed by the official doctrine of Socialist Realism or unofficial anti-Soviet dissent, young writers in Russia today must search the current confusion for themes that resonate successfully with their own personal, internal voice. In the new generation of writers to which Arbatova, Gremina, and Mikhailova belong, there is a greater consciousness of belonging to European literary and theatrical traditions. At the same time, they remain very much products of their own society and culture. Despite tremendous variations of plot and style, the creative confluence of these writers is encoded in an exchange present in all three plays: an offhand comment on the fact that England is an island, and it must be awful to live in such an enclosed space. This remark sounds especially ironic in the mouth of Sashenka, the young man who is imprisoned for years behind the mirror in Catherine the Great's reception-hall (in Gremina's *Behind the Mirror*), but the ubiquitousness of this remark indicates a common attitude: whatever the discomforts of home, for the Russian, the West provokes a sense of danger unfathomable to the Western mind.

With the possible exception of Maria Arbatova, who is, in fact, president of the liberal feminist organization "Harmony," the reader may be hard-pressed to discern any "feminist" trend in a contemporary Western sense among the writings of contemporary Russian women in general. Indeed, the "woman's lot" in twentieth-century Russia has been shaped by an odd admixture of loudly vaunted "Socialist Equality" between the sexes and domestic "Domostroi" (the medieval domestic legal code). For women writers, this has meant that opportunities for professional advancement according to individual merit have been vitiated by a pervasive unofficial dismissive attitude towards "ladies'" [damskie] literary products. In the 1980s, however, writers such as Liudmila Petrushevskaia and Liudmila Razumovskaia revealed the strains and tears in the fabric of society in an un-compromisingly, decidedly "unfeminine" manner, causing the magazine *Soviet Theater* to declare in 1986 that "a genuine crusade of women onto the Soviet stage" was in process.

These writers' dark vision of contemporary Russian reality was, in turn, cast off by the younger generation of writers, just as their contemporaries cast off an outmoded political and economic system. The writers in this volume have man-aged to bridge successfully the topical and the eternal, masculine and feminine, Russian and Western perspectives. At the center of each play is a highly original romantic conflict that is simultaneously a conflict of cultural value systems. The resolution of these interpenetrating cultural and emotional conflicts is tragicomic and multifaceted.

Although virtually unknown in the English-speaking world, these writers are frequently mentioned among the "rising stars" of their generation, and have found eager audiences in Western Europe: Olga Mikhailova's play *A Holiday* was made into a film (*Rez-de-Chaussée* by Igor Minaev) which won recognition in Cannes; Elena Gremina's and Maria Arbatova's plays have been broadcast on German radio. Arbatova's plays *Session in a Communal Apartment* and *Equation with Two Knowns* have been staged in amateur productions in England and the United States respectively. This volume aims to give these writers the broader exposure they deserve in the new post-perestroika process of cultural interaction.

During the late 1980s, the "iron curtain" separating Russia from the rest of Europe and the United States dropped, making travel to the West not only poss-ible, but the seeming realization of many dreams come true. Simultaneously, writers, film and television cameras focussed on the negative economic and polit-ical conditions at home. Young Russians in ever-increasing numbers went off to seek their fortunes in the West. While many such voyages met with success, nostalgia for the Motherland was omnipresent, and indeed many voyagers dis-covered that life in the West did not deliver its bounty without many hardships hitherto undreamed of. Maria Arbatova's play, *On the Road to Ourselves* deftly captures through her central characters experiences typical of many. The play presents the parallel searches of two Russian emigrants, Tanya and Yevgeny, who find, lose, and find each other again in the "through the looking-glass" world of Amsterdam. The play is at once delightfully satiric of contemporary Western values, and painfully revelatory of the dilemmas facing young Russians today, when "to emigrate or not to emigrate" is one of the major "cursed questions" of their existence. While Tanya, a single mother driven to improve her own and her family's material lot, encounters other fortune-hunters from the former Russian empire, Yevgeny hungers for an intellectual link and stumbles into contact with followers of Rudolph Steiner, whose philosophy of anthroposophy strongly influenced Russian artistic, literary, and philosophical thought in the early twen-tieth century. Yevgeny's search unmasks much of the hypocrisy in the "free" Western search for self.

Arbatova's concerns for such issues as individual rights, equality of the sexes and medical care place her in the mainstream of Western humanist values. Her political activism lends her plays an immediate connection with American and British audiences; her underlying "Russianness" gives new dimensions to familiar problems. Arbatova's heroines may strive for independence and self-realization, yet they continue to find themselves incomplete without fulfillment of their romantic aspirations. It is this central romantic yearning that separates Arbatova's work from its Western feminist counterparts. *On the Road to Ourselves* was originally commissioned as part of a "New Artists" Series at the Organic Theater in Chicago on the basis of a scene from Arbatova's earlier work, *Drang nach Westen*.

Elena Gremina, on the other hand, finds her inspiration predominantly in the Russian past, combining compelling historical plots with ever new territory of associative cultural meaning. Her first major play, *The Wheel of Fortune*, examined a contemporary family's efforts to find meaningful lives in the present, only to find true meaning in retreat to values of the past. *The Cornet "O" Affair*, set on the eve of the Russian Revolution, revisited a criminal investigation of a fatal passion. *Behind the Mirror* retreats to the eighteenth century, but also finds there a meeting place of contemporary and eternal conflicts. Gremina's story is based on documented facts, and uses material from Catherine's well-known correspondence with Friedrich Melchior Grimm, German born publisher of the French *philosophes*, as a frame for the psychological comedy-drama of the three main characters: Catherine the Great ("Matushka" or "Little Mother" of Russia), Lieutenant Alexander Lanskoy ("Sashenka," an affectionate diminutive of Aleksander), and Lady Bruce, who serves both Catherine and Catherine's former lover and political advisor, Prince Potemkin ("His Highness"). Only three characters appear on stage, but myriad allusions to Catherine's contemporaries create a backdrop of complex political and social intrigue. Potemkin never appears on stage, but it is his political maneuvers which move the plot.

Gremina's heroine, Catherine the Great, is seen divested of her regal splendor. Though intellectually and physically titanic, this Catherine is curiously vulnerable to the simplicity of true love. The young officer who comes to "serve" his Tsarina, Sashenka, is linked folklorically to the Russian fairy-tale hero, Ivanuska-Durachok, or Ivan the Fool, who, despite his seeming helplessness, understands and attains more than his stronger, handsomer, smarter elder brothers. While he is Catherine's true love, he is also her ideological opponent, rejecting the scientific attainments of the enlightenment (knowledge of geography, medicine), believing instead in superstition and trusting the fate that is inscribed in the palm of his hand. Catherine, German princess become Tsarina of Russia, encounters the mystery of the land she rules incarnate in this simple young man. *Behind the Mirror* recently became a major box-office hit at the Moscow Art Theater, with opera singer Galina Vishnevskaya in the lead.

While the third playwright in this volume, Olga Mikhailova, writes ever of the present, she frequently brings old literary types to new life, reinforcing the contemporaneity in classical conflicts of love and death. Her first major success, *A Holiday*, was a thinly veiled retelling of the tragic love story between Carmen and Don José. The hero of *Russian Dream* is a contemporary version of the beloved

Ilya Ilyich Oblomov, the lethargic hero of Ivan Goncharov's nineteenth-century novel, who inspired the radical critic Nikolai Dobroliubov to diagnose as "Oblomovitis" the malady affecting the Russian gentry of his day. Mikhailova, however, does not diagnose; she playfully intertwines social commentary and literary allusions in a contemporary "fairy tale." In Russian fairy tales, three is a magic number; and three meetings of the hero and heroine—at the beginning, middle and end of the 1980s—provide the structure of *Russian Dream*. The setting is a communal apartment. In this most prosaic of settings, Mikhailova posits the magical meeting of a "princess from a far-off kingdom" and the quintessential "Russian at a Rendezvous," (another nineteenth-century diagnosis of Russian male impotence by the radical critic Chernyshevsky).

Mikhailova's play, while focussing on a love story, surreptitiously charts the changes occuring in Russia during the 1980s. Her Ilya Ilyich, while reincarnating a familiar nineteenth-century hero, represents a familiar type of contemporary Russian: the young intellectual, oblivious of the world without, yet highly observant of the world within, vaguely conscious of just how deeply his being is rooted in his own culture. While his physical survival seems precarious, his spiritual survival is assured by his "eternal Russian" nature. The heroine of *Russian Dream* has been presented here as American, but in other versions she has been easily "translated" into a French or German one. It is not nationality that is the issue, but the romantic confrontation between Russia and the West. *Russian Dream* has been staged in French at the Mayakovsky Theater in Moscow and in English by the "Horizontal Eight" Players of Toronto, Canada.

The reader/audience of the plays in *Russian Mirror* share with the dramatis personae of all three works an encounter with worlds and character types that may initially appear as foreign. It is hoped that, in living with them through the short space of the play, all will come to recognize the ultimate universality of the human experience reflected here.

A Note on Russian Names in the Texts

Russian names have been known to confuse the English-speaking reader. The following is offered as a brief guide.

The formal (respectful) form of address in Russian is not by title and last name (i.e., Mr., Mrs. Gorbachev), but by first name and patronymic (middle name formed from taking the father's first name and adding a suffix -ovich/-evich for a man, -ovna/-evna for a woman).

Last names have both masculine and feminine forms:

Lev Nikolaevich Tolstoy (= son of Nikolai);
Sofia Andreevna Tolstaia (= daughter of Andrei).

In informal address, the first name is rarely used without making it diminutive. Normally, a close acquaintance would use the form of the first name that ends in -ya. Suffixes such as -usha, -unya, -enka, -ka add varying degrees of emotional coloration. Therefore, Ivan Denisovich (formal address) would be known to his friends as Vanya, Vanka, Vaniusha, Vanenka, etc.

Common names, including those occurring in this volume, are:
  Alexander/Alexandra = Sasha, Sanya, Sanka, Sashunya, Sashulya, Shura.
  Yevgeny/Evgenia = Zhenya, Zhenka, etc.
  Ilya = Iliusha, Iliushenka, etc.
  Georgii = Zhora, Gosha
  Natalia = Natasha, Nata, Natusya, Natka, etc.
  Olga = Olya, Olenka, Oliushka
  Tatiana = Tanya, Taniusha, etc.
  Vladimir = Volodya, Vova, Vovochka, etc.

In Maria Arbatova's *On the Road to Ourselves*, the characters' names reflect their ethnic identity. Any Russian would immediately recognize Tanya and Yevgeny as the twice-thwarted lovers in the nineteenth-century classic verse novel *Eugene Onegin*. Stephanie pretends to be a Polish princess, but Polish and Ukrainian names are very close, and as she points out, in her Ukrainian village there were several women by the same name. The Mongol's name, Badbayar, sounds both typical and parodic at the same time.

Behind the Mirror features the Russian Empress, Catherine the Great. As Tsarina, Catherine was officially "Mother to All Russians", hence she is referred to as Matushka ("mother" + "ushka"). While she nicknamed her former lovers by title or references to classical mythology, her decision to call Alexander Lanskoy "Sashenka" reveals (as does the nightcap she wears in the opening scene) her yearning for a simpler, more domestic intimacy than she has previously experienced, as well as reflecting a maternal affection for the young Russian man who is appointed as her lover. The names Matushka and Sashenka are both stressed on the first syllable.

Melissa T. Smith

Maria Arbatova

Maria Arbatova

ON THE ROAD TO OURSELVES

A play-voyage

DRAMATIS PERSONAE

TANYA
YEVGENY
STEPHANIE
HERBERT
ANITA
CHRISTOPHER
BADBAYAR
ELENA
MARTIN
JAQUELINE
RICHARD

A compartment on a inter-city train. Yevgeny is sitting by the window, absorbed in a thick advertising newspaper. Tanya enters, dragging a huge suitcase.

TANYA. Guten Tag. Khello!

Yevgeny looks up from his newspaper, looks at her with evident irritation, and again buries himself in his newspaper. She sits opposite him.

TANYA. (*Depicting a strained gaiety and ease*). Khello!
YEVGENY. (*not looking up from his newspaper*). Khello!

She gets a mirror out of her handbag, fixes her makeup, and assumes an excessively inviting pose.

TANYA. (*actively gesticulating*). I em Rushen. I em toorist. Understand? No? Oh, God, I studied English in school... School! Schule! Understand?

Yevgeny puts his newspaper aside, observes Tanya for a long time, and grins.

YEVGENY. I speak Russkii.
TANYA. Great! You're German, right? Berlin is a terrific place! I strolled about a lot, while I was changing trains. Yeh, blow me away. But, maybe you're Dutch. You have guldens there?
YEVGENY. Ameriken...Orizona.
TANYA. American? Oy! It's not possible! My life dream (*sings*) Ameriken boiy, Ameriken boiy, uyedu s toboy!
YEVGENY. (*smiles*). My naim iz Dzhonnie. Starr. I am work in Orizona ooniversitat. I am professor Rushen literatoor.
TANYA. A professor! (*nearly faints from happiness, lights up a cigarette, pulls together all her conceptions about how to interact with the professorate, pulls her skirt up closer to her knees*). My name is Tanya. Tatiana, a Russian soul...More than anything else in school I loved literature, really! Katerina, a ray of light in the Kingdom of darkness[1] "Fathers and Sons in Turgenev's novel *Fathers and Sons.* " How does it go:
> Unmindful of the proud world's pleasure
> But friendship's claim alone in view
> I wish I could have brought a treasure
> Far worthier to pledge to you
... and so forth.[2]
YEVGENY. Oh!

---

[1]The heroine of *The Thunderstorm* by Ostrovsky (19th century). Tanya cites the cliche about the heroine taken from the interpretation of the 19th-century radical critic N. Dobroliubov. This and succeeding literature quotes represent cliched exam topics every Soviet schoolchild knows.
[2]Dedication to Pushkin's *Eugene Onegin* trans. Walter Arndt. New York: E.P. Dutton, 1963, p. 1, ©Ardis Publishers, Dana Point, CA. reprinted here with permission of publisher.

3

TANYA. The entire class used to copy my compositions. Yes. I even wanted to go to journalism school, but life dictated otherwise, and I went into engineering (technical school). You know, Johnny, that has its romantic side as well, "reinforced concrete construction and bridges"...

YEVGENY. Oh, I no understand...Reinforce concrete...?

TANYA. That's OK, not even Russians can pronounce it. I'm so tired, Johnny, of our institute...I work in a research institute, helping science progress. I so wanted to see the world. So, you see, I took a vacation, I'm going to see my girlfriend. She married a real ticket.

YEVGENY. A ticket? No understand.

TANYA. A Dutchman. True, he's already getting along in years... But she's happy.

Pause.

YEVGENY. Taneeya...

TANYA. Yes?

YEVGENY. You legs beautiful.

TANYA. (*freezes from the unexpectedness of the remark*). My legs are OK.

Pause.

You know, I checked out those German girls in Berlin. Awful frights.

YEVGENY. Oh, I no understand. Fright...?

TANYA. Well, awful, ugly. Not beautiful in face. Russian girls beautiful, but German girls, no beautiful. Understand?

YEVGENY. Yes, I understand.

TANYA. No, you don't. You come to our country, see for yourself.

YEVGENY. I very want Russia. I always dream have tourism Russia. Russia is slavyankii fairytale.

TANYA. Fairytale! Horror story! You come, Johnny, I'll put you up. I'll show you everything. You know, Moscow...Boulevards... I bet in America you don't have boulevards.

YEVGENY. Boolvar? What is Boolvar?

TANYA. Well, trees grow along it. Trees, trees. Big old trees.

YEVGENY. Forest? In Boolvar is living wild animals?

TANYA. What animals? You crazy? Animals live in a zoo.

Pause.

Johnny, are you married?

YEVGENY. Menya wife Sally dead. Catastrof. He sit car, little heroin. You understand? Heroin. Narcotics.

TANYA. Narcotics? This is really something!

YEVGENY. Y-Yess. Narcotics. She were young girl.

TANYA. So you're completely alone?

YEVGENY. Allown, Taneeya. I all allown.

TANYA. And where are you going?

YEVGENY. I camed from Berlin-ooniversitat. I have read lecshun. I go Eton-ooniversitat. I am like England. For me hard Amerika with no my Sally.

TANYA. How's that? England is, well, on an island.

YEVGENY. Hook van Holland goes boat England. Beeg boat. Boat with bar, swimming pool, casino.

TANYA. A steamship? Yes?

YEVGENY. Steamship, Taneeya.

TANYA. Oy, just once to travel by steamship! And does it fit many people on board?

YEVGENY. Many, Taneeya.

TANYA. Well, five hundred? A thousand?

YEVGENY. Yes, thousand.

TANYA. A thousand, and all foreigners!

Pause.

Johnny, you're so sweet...

YEVGENY. Taneeya, I want veeski. I have go to bar.

TANYA. *(scared)*. To what bar? You want to go out?

YEVGENY. Bar is in another car.

TANYA. Bar on an inter-city train? Well, this is really something! They do live it up, the scum!

YEVGENY. I no understand, Taneeya, what is - scum?

TANYA. I just made a play on words, Johnny. You understand?

YEVGENY. *(Shrugs his shoulders)*. Understand.

Goes to the door.

TANYA. John, you're not afraid I'll run away with your bag?

YEVGENY. What is "run away with bag?"

TANYA. A joke. A play on words. I'll wait for you, Johnny *(blows him a kiss)*.

He leaves. She quickly takes out her cosmetics, hysterically begins to put on mascara.

TANYA. Idiot! You unwashed idiot! Anka told me to "always be in shape!" A professor, shit! Not married! Walks right into my arms! Almost hooked him! Shit! Almost hooked a professor on my first try! Of course, American women, they're all frigid! Frights, like German women! I wonder, if I let him screw me right now, will I scare him off or not? I wish I had could ask somebody's advice! I don't know anything about Americans, the girls only told me about Dutchmen! Main thing is to be as sexy as possible! I'll sit like this, with my legs on the table. Twenty minutes of looking at my legs and he'll marry me. Damn! I've got Soviet underwear on, as soon as he sees it, he'll turn impotent! Anka told me: put on your best, your co-op undies! And always be in shape! But I put it in my suitcase, so as not to wear it out while traveling. Idiot! Better no bra at all, than a Soviet one! *(Pulls her bra out from under her blouse, fearfully looking at the door)*. Oh, swell! A couple of buttons to undo! Panties! I've got to change my panties! *(scrunches up the bra, hides it in her suitcase, kicks off her shoes, pulls down her panty-hose on one side. pulls off her panties on one leg, looking around at the door, pulls on the panty-hose on that leg, puts on her shoe, tries to do the same on the other leg, but here he enters with a bottle and plastic cups; she freezes, pulls her skirt down on her knees and scrunches up in the corner)*. Johnny, so fast? There wasn't any line?

5

YEVGENY. What is line?

TANYA. Whiskey? Great! Is it more like vodka or straight spirits?

YEVGENY. (*shrugs his shoulders, extends a glass with whiskey to her*) You very pretty woman, Taneeya.

TANYA. (*smiles, drinks*). Oh, how bitter! John, you want me to get drunk, right?

YEVGENY. It only is little veeski, Taneeya.

TANYA. Imagine, "only little;" that's quite a bottle!

Pause.

YEVGENY. Taneeya, I want sleep with you.

She turns to stone.

I want have you… woman. Understand?

She shakes her head in dismay.

One hundred dollars, Taneeya.

She once again shakes her head and looks at him, insulted; he sits next to her and starts to embrace her.

TANYA. John! (*jumps up out of his embrace and sits across from him*) You probably decided that I'm a prostitute, right? That you can behave this way with me? That you can have me for a hundred dollars? Yes? Because I'm Russian? Yes? You decided that?

YEVGENY. Oh, sorry Taneeya. I have not to offense Tanya.

TANYA. That means with Russians you can do anything you want? Because they haven't seen the great wide world? Because they're beggars? You have to marry American women, but you can have Russians in a train compartment for a hundred dollars? Yes?

YEVGENY. Oh, Taneeya, forgive me, Taneeya. I no want offend, Taneeya. Train morning Rotterdam. Taneeya go out. I no more see Taneeya.

TANYA. Oh, why not? I could come to see you in England. I haven't ever been to England! I haven't ever been anywhere, John! They never let us out before! We lived like in a prison!

YEVGENY. Oh, I know. I read.

TANYA. I, you might say, have come to take a look at the world, meet new people, and you with your "hundred dollars!"

YEVGENY. Oh, no Taneeya. At home in Ameriken this normal. Dollar is dollar. Love is love. It is no offense, Taneeya.

TANYA. But would you marry a woman you slept with in a train for a hundred dollars?

YEVGENY. Y-yes. Dollar -- is dollar. Love—is love. You to me very beautiful, Taneeya.

TANYA. And does your mummy think the same way?

YEVGENY. What is mummy?

TANYA. Mama, mother!

YEVGENY. Menya muzzer live Kentooky with new young husband.

Pause.

TANYA. Johnny, I really don't know what to do. It's so unexpected, in general…, well, I don't know what to say to you.

YEVGENY(*takes her by the hand*). Say, say, Taneeya!

TANYA. (*thinks for a long time, then, with eyes cast down*). Well, if this is normal in your country, then I agree…

Pause.

For a hundred dollars.

He takes her by the knees and, caressing her legs, makes his way up to her skirt, she squeezes her skirt with her hands.

TANYA. Johnny, you know what, I've got to go out! Just wait a minute, I have to go out on the platform! Just to fix something!

YEVGENY. Later, Taneeya…, later… Wait… Taneeya…

In a struggle alternating with passionate caresses; she is the victor.

YEVGENY. (*breathing heavily*). In the next car, near the bar. (*Indicates the direction with his hand*)

TANYA. What?

YEVGENY. What you want, Taneeya.

TANYA. What do you mean? They have toilets on inter-city trains? You must be kidding! Senk you my luff (*runs out, sidling backwards*).

He wipes the sweat off his forehead, screws the top on the whiskey bottle, sticks the bottle in his bag, then packs her bag into his bag, looks at himself in the mirror, straightens his hair, takes his bag and her suitcase and quickly exits. The compartment is empty, only the sound of the wheels and the announcements made by sweet-voiced Dutch women at the stations, which are close together.

The door opens. She looks in and immediately disappears. Then one more time. After a bit she enters and looks around in surprise.

TANYA. This seems to be the right compartment. (*takes in her hands the newspaper he left behind, and finally, realizing what has happened, drops the newspaper.*) Mama! What should I do now? (*weeps, yells*) Emergency cord! Have to pull the emergency cord! How do you say "thief" in English? To the police! They have police! They'll have to give me an interpreter! It's obligatory! (*throwing open the doors*) Khelp me! Khelp me! (*standing for a minute without any answer, sits down, and wails*). The train made a stop! It's night! They don't have a chance in hell of finding him! It's all over! I'm screwed! I'm lost! It's just as mother said. A fool here is the same fool there! Oh, Lord! What should I do? I borrowed a hundred thousand to get hard currency, and for the tickets, and clothes, and presents! I'll never be able to pay it all back, never! And mother's ill! I have to pay for my daughter's music lessons! It's all over! I'm screwed!

She lies on the seat face downward and lies there motionless for a few minutes. Then gets up, looks at herself for a long time in the mirror, weaves her hair into a braid, looks at herself, unbraids it, rubs her makeup off her cheeks a bit. Remains pleased with her looks. Takes off her leather belt, tests it for durability, looks at herself in the mirror for a long time. Then looks out the window. Wincing, she drinks the rest of the whiskey. Throws off her shoes, and begins to fit the belt to the upper luggage rack. Having tied and adjusted the belt, she sits down, lights up a cigarette, looks out the window.

TANYA. (*mournfully sings*) Oy, da ne vecher da ne vecher.../ Mne maly-malo spalos'/ Mne maly-malo spalos'/ Oy da vo sne prividelos'[1]

Wipes away her tears, blows her nose into the wind-curtain on the window, checks her make-up again, as if it had importance, gets up, measures the noose, looks in the mirror again. The door opens, he enters with the suitcase and bag. Sits down.

Long pause.

TANYA. (*hoarsely*) Where's my purse?

He drags over his bag, gets her purse out of it, throws on the seat.

TANYA. (*furiously*). Where did you go with my things! American louse! You took it into the next car for a piss? Yes?

She grabs the newspaper and starts with all her might to pound his face with it.

TANYA. Sleazebag! Rotten sleaze! He's a professor? Do all professors in America rip off suitcases?!

YEVGENY. (*shields himself against her with his arms, then pushes her so that she flies against the wall*). Idiot, I'm as much an American as you are!

She is struck dumb. Pause

YEVGENY. What are you goggling at me for? Ach, how we are deceived in our pure intentions! We were ready to pop our cherry for a hundred dollars, and our suitcase is almost stolen! Ay, ay, ay! At the sight of a pair of American pants we spread our legs and they, the nasty things, won't marry us after that!

TANYA. (*quietly*). I'll turn you over to the police!

YEVGENY. Idiot, where will you turn me over to? Your English isn't enough to ask "Where's the bathroom?" You should fall down at my feet for bringing your junk back to you, and you make goat-faces at me!

---

[1]"The Dream of Stenka Razin:" a folk-song made popular by Zhanna Bichevskaya (a Joan Baez-type folk singer). In it, a gypsy interprets the dream and predicts the death of Razin.

TANYA. Thank you, darling, for changing your mind about stealing my suitcase! Thank you, my dearest! I spent five years saving up for this trip, I'm up to my eyeballs in debt! I'm going to be paying it back for the rest of my life, in order to give it to some goat on the way! My mother has half her stomach removed! My daughter in the third grade has all kinds of food allergies! If I don't cook up some guldens in Holland, it's curtains for all of us! I don't have anything! Not an apartment, or a profession, or a man, or my health! My daughter has grown up in hand-me-downs! Mother is growing old from life in a communal apartment! I can't live this way anymore! *(she weeps)*. What am I guilty of? That I bore a child, and don't know how to steal? Is that it?

YEVGENY. Get down off your soap-box. A person has to learn to respect himself, then he'll get the life he deserves.

TANYA. And where could I have learned that? My father abandoned us, I wasn't even a year old! My mother called me nothing but a degenerate throughout my childhood. When I was thirteen our alcoholic neighbor raped me, and since then I've been afraid to tell my mother. Until I was twenty I was afraid to enter the apartment without her, afraid the neighbor would hit on me. I came here to learn how to respect myself...

YEVGENY. You really found where to come to. I've been hanging around here for three years, you see how I've come to respect myself. I respected myself as far as stealing your suitcase.

Pause.

TANYA. So you were putting the moves on me only to rip me off? Why did you barge in like that?

Pause.

YEVGENY. No, I really wanted to fuck you. But then, if you had gone along, I would have...

TANYA. Well, you're a real prick!

YEVGENY. Well, if I had said I was a Russian, you would have immediately skipped off to another compartment.

TANYA. I didn't come here for a Russian!

YEVGENY. My wife's just the same kind! Lives with a black dick and makes believe she's happy...

TANYA. So you should take revenge on your wife, not me.

Pause.

YEVGENY. But why did you skip out so early? Maybe I wouldn't have wanted to leave afterward.

Pause.

TANYA. Well, I had to.

Pause.

Well, I thought that you were an American, and I have Sov panties on. Well, I wanted to change them while you had gone to the bar, but I didn't manage to in time. I'd taken them off one leg, but not the other. Did you notice?

YEVGENY. No. But an American would have found it a real trip, at least something new. For every colored person there they have disposable underwear with a computer!

TANYA. You see, all the more reason! A professor, I thought. An American...

YEVGENY. Idiot, they call any teacher there professor. You're an engineer, they'd call you a professor there, too.

TANYA. I'm not an engineer. I'm just a lab assistant in a research institute. I was laid off. At the employment office they proposed I study to become a bookkeeper. But I can't stand it. I'm better off with a bucket and a rag. I cleaned and cleaned. And I have heart problems. That's the whole sad song.

YEVGENY. And you, like a babe, thought that all American professors are just waiting for Moscow cleaning-women?

TANYA. No, now really! He wanted to rob me, then for good measure fuck me, and what's more for kickers give me a lecture on morality!

YEVGENY. Idiot, you owe me a drink for the training. If not me then one of them will deal with you a lot rougher. You just keep coming, you think just once of pouring water instead of gas, and they catch you for it then hit it rich! They've studied this for a thousand years. They have marriage contracts made up by lawyers so that you won't have to divide up the spoons and sheets later! A professor will marry her! How about that!

TANYA. (*Takes her purse, digs around in it, gets a couple of pills, puts them in her mouth.*) Bring me some water.

YEVGENY. Why have you gotten so pale, Tanya?

TANYA. (*with pills in her mouth, as if shriveled up*) Bring me some water.

YEVGENY. (*grabs a glass, rushes around*). You lie down, just lie down a bit... Let's put your purse under your head... I'll be right back. (*runs out*).

She lies down, looks with an empty sick expression.

YEVGENY. (*running in*). Here, drink this. How are you, Tanya? There's going to be a station soon. Let's get it off. You can get off at every stop here. We'll find a doctor. The doctors here are really something, you know.

TANYA. The doctors here cost guldens. Never mind, I'll feel better.

YEVGENY. (*sits down next to her*) Is your hair natural or dyed?

TANYA. Natural.

YEVGENY. Cool.

TANYA. So gorgeous, that you ran off with my suitcase?

YEVGENY. So gorgeous that I came back with your suitcase.

TANYA. What have you been doing robbing Sovs on trains for three years?

YEVGENY. I, by the way, never robbed anyone.

TANYA. Really?

YEVGENY. With three languages I carried sacks in Germany, washed dishes, then I...cracked up. Started to drink, almost drank up everything. They say in Amsterdam it's easier to get by. Feeling better, eh?

TANYA. When I take two tablets, I feel better immediately.

Pause.

YEVGENY. I picked the emptiest compartment so as not to see anybody, I was feeling really shitty. Besides us here, there are only two black woman snoozing at the other end. And you barge in: all yours for a hundred dollars!

TANYA. Do you at least understand how much fruit I can buy my little girl for those dollars? Multiply it by the exchange rate!

YEVGENY. Then it suddenly came into my head: I'll fuck her, and then slip off with her bag full of hard currency, to cool off the American dream. And then I opened your suitcase, and there was your bra all rolled up. I took it in my hand and it... was still warm... I could go crazy. And one strap was sewn on with black thread.

TANYA. (*indignant*) There isn't any white thread in the stores! Well, where could I find it!?

YEVGENY. You know, German women, they're completely different. Back home, you know, every sales-girl is waiting for a prince, and here every hippie counts her money. It's true! If my wife had loved me, I would have built Berlin for her in Moscow!

TANYA. I heard that before from a guy.

YEVGENY. And you?

TANYA. Me? I came here.

YEVGENY. Why didn't you love him?

TANYA. I don't know. Probably I'm not capable of it, so I didn't love him.

Pause.

YEVGENY. I was invited to enter a graduate program! I was the best student in my group... Yeh, I didn't need your suitcase. What's in it? Vodka, caviar, try getting rid of them later! I needed your purse with hard currency! Why did I grab your suitcase?

TANYA. But how did you catch up with the train after that? I mean, when you... well, when you started to feel sorry for me?

YEVGENY. Idiot! I just moved over into the next car. You wouldn't have figured that out for your life!

Pause.

TANYA. If you call me an idiot one more time, I'll smack you...

Pause.

YEVGENY. Tanya...

Pause.

TANYA. Well?

Pause.

YEVGENY. May I kiss you?

Pause.

TANYA. Okay.

They kiss. The train wheels clack on, and past the windows in darkness as before, whiz picturesque Dutch houses with great big glowing windows.

* * *

Living-room in a well-to-do Dutch house. Several tasteless paintings, everything irreproachable. STEPHANIE in a luxurious peignoir is lying on the sofa with a glass in her hand. TANYA sits across from her on the rug. She has bought new clothes on sale and has dyed her hair some god-awful color.

STEPHANIE. Pour me another.

TANYA. *(jumps up to the bar)* Whiskey?

STEPHANIE. Listen, you've been loafing around her for a week already, are you really not capable of learning, for the guldens I pay you, that I can't stand that American slop?

TANYA. *(goes to her with a bottle of vodka, smiling flatteringly, pours Stephanie a drink).* Forgive me, Stephanie, I just can't get used to the idea that a Polish princess drinks vodka!

STEPHANIE. I need someone who gets used to things in a hurry. Don't pour much. A glass should never be very full. It's better if you get up again. So, tell me more.

TANYA. *(puts the bottle on the bar, sits in her former position).* And when I woke up, he wasn't in the compartment any more.

STEPHANIE. And your things?

TANYA. They were all in place. And there was a note on the pillow. "You're the best woman I have ever known, but we'd never be able to survive here together." And a hundred marks. *(cries.)*

STEPHANIE. Why a hundred marks? You'd agreed to a hundred dollars! A dollar is more than a mark.

TANYA. *(wiping her nose with her sleeve)* Stephanie, what do you mean, we agreed? It wasn't with him that I'd made the agreement! He just left it!

STEPHANIE: What do you mean, not with him? What happened, another guy came along?

TANYA. Stephanie, when we made the agreement, I thought he was an American!

STEPHANIE. That's his problem. He had a woman, he should pay as stipulated. This isn't *Russland*! Don't wipe your nose on your sleeve, take a handkerchief.

TANYA. *(Takes a handkerchief, twirls it around her hand, makes it into a dove)* Stephanie, is it possible to find him?

STEPHANIE. *(laughs)* Of course! Advertise in the evening paper: Russian who fucked me in the Berlin-Rotterdam train for a hundred marks, I'll be waiting for you every day at two o'clock on Rembrant Platz!"

TANYA. I want to find him.

STEPHANIE. What? He was such a classy guy?

TANYA. You want some more vodka?

STEPHANIE. Please.

Tanya throws her paper dove on the side of the bar, stands up, pours Stephanie vodka.

STEPHANIE. Pick up the paper. I don't like paper lying around. I like things neat.

Tanya picks up the dove, crumples it, puts it in her pocket.

STEPHANIE. Three languages, a good fuck... He won't starve to death in Amsterdam. He'll hire himself out to some old lady twice a week.

TANYA. Him?

STEPHANIE. (*laughs*) I see he hasn't taught you anything with your suitcase! And, by the way, how come you've settled yourself so comfortably? Have you done the dishes?

TANYA. (*gets up*). I have.

STEPHANIE. In the dishwasher?

TANYA. Yes.

STEPHANIE. Look, if I see you washing them under the faucet again, I'll take it out of your pay. I told you, water is expensive! You aren't in Russland.

TANYA. I washed them in the dishwasher.

STEPHANIE. And did you clean the stained-glass windows?

TANYA. I cleaned them this morning.

STEPHANIE. With new polish?

TANYA. Yes.

STEPHANIE. And where's the old?

TANYA. It ran out.

STEPHANIE. I had a girl named Lena before you. From Kharkov. It lasted her ten days.

TANYA. I'll try. And why did that Lena leave you?

STEPHANIE. Lena? Girls usually don't stay with me for more than ten days.

TANYA. (*smiling*) That means I have three days left?

STEPHANIE. There's hundreds of you. I call the agency, and ask them to send a new one. They pick you up right off the train, they can tell by the eyes.

Pause.

TANYA. Has Mister Julian gone out on business?

STEPHANIE. And why do you ask?

TANYA. It's just that without him you've become ... completely different, Stephanie.

STEPHANIE. Julian's gone off to his old whore and his son. Sometimes he spends the night there, and I get to relax.

PARROT. (*in a cage*) Get out, get out, get out, bitches!

TANYA. (*jumps up*) I get so scared with he screeches!

STEPHANIE. Cover that creature with a cloth! No, not with that one!

TANYA. (*covers the cage with a scarf*). I didn't know that Mister Julian had a son.

STEPHANIE. A goat just like his father. And he's leaving all this to him! (*gestures to the walls*). If I, fool that I am, hadn't had so many abortions, all this would be mine. He could croak tomorrow and I'll be left again bare-assed!

TANYA. Maybe I don't understand anything, but you, Stephanie, with your heritage! And your looks!

STEPHANIE. Pour me some more vodka.

TANYA. (*jumps up, pours vodka*). I'm just so thrilled by you all the time. You have taken me in and warmed me in you home. I thought it was dog-eat-dog here. My girl-friend told me so much...

STEPHANIE. They are beasts. Most beastly beasts. I spilled so much sweat and blood here.

TANYA. Tell me about it, Stephanie.

STEPHANIE. Bring me an orange.

Tanya runs out, returns with an orange.

STEPHANIE. No, not that kind. I don't eat that kind. Find one that has a thinner skin. And peel it.

Tanya runs out, returns with an orange, peels it with her fingers.

STEPHANIE. (*with disgust*) Serve it on a fruit plate. With a fruit knife and fork!

Tanya runs out, returns with the orange on a plate, with a knife and fork.

STEPHANIE. (*takes it in her hands, then tosses it away*) Blockhead! This is a fish knife and fork! It's the same thing over and over again!

TANYA. (*picks it up off the floor in tears*) Forgive me, Stephanie...

Goes to the kitchen. Returns with a plate, knife, and fork.

TANYA. I washed it. Maybe I should peel a new one?

STEPHANIE. Enough, already, give me that one. (*eats the orange*). And take one for yourself, since we've started on a spree. Only with a thick skin. They're cheaper. And eat with a knife and fork.

TANYA. Thanks. (*exits, returns with an orange, knife, and fork, sits on the rug, picks at it with the fruit knife in imitation of Stephanie*). But Mr. Julian eats fruit without a knife and fork...

STEPHANIE. Well, he's the swine of swine in general. He stirs his coffee in the morning with a ball-point pen, then licks it and sticks it in his pocket. In seven years I haven't been able to retrain him.

TANYA. Mr. Julian is so nice, so rich! You're so lucky, even though he's old.

STEPHANIE. Ha, ha, ha! Lucky! I've put in seven years, and he's still willing everything to his son as before! And just try dropping a hint! I have to account for every single button I buy, explain every chocolate bar. That's the way they do things, the motherf... You know how much money he has? You haven't even dreamed of such figures! And he explains to me that I have to buy cosmetics wholesale! You understand?

TANYA. No.

STEPHANIE. Look here, I could just drop by an expensive store, buy myself some face cream for ten guldens, toss it in my purse and walk away like a normal person. But no, I have to run around and think about where I can buy three jars of this cream for ten guldens! I'm forty-five years old, and still I should run around on errands?

TANYA. But it's better to get three jars for the same price, isn't it?

STEPHANIE. Tanya, that's it! You're a dunce! You with your Sov psychology will never get anywhere! Get along home, kid! There's a different principle here: say you're going to have a million, and you'll have one!

TANYA. How's that?

STEPHANIE. That, Tanya, cannot be taught. If you're not born with it, you'll die without it.

TANYA. But Stephanie, I'm a good learner.

STEPHANIE. Pour me another vodka. (*Tanya pours*). To tell the truth, I'm from a Ukrainian village myself. It's called Raigorod. You understand? Raigorod.

TANYA. What? So all that about your grandfather from Warsaw... About your estate...

STEPHANIE. I'm as much a princess as you are! I'm a Hunkie! About half the population of Raigorod has Polish last names. Stepanida Gusinskaya. And across the fence lived another Styopka Gusinskaya. And down by headquarters lived another one! It was through connections in Odessa that I got my passport changed to say that I am Stephanie, and that I'm Polish.

TANYA. Is it really possible to have your nationality changed in your passport?

STEPHANIE. For money you can do anything... My mother was from the country, but she got me from some Leningrad veterinarian who knocked her up. That's why I have such fine bones. I was a rare bird in the village. In Odessa I got into a medical-technical school. Then worked as a nurse on a ship. Do you know what it's like working there? Do it with everyone, just make sure each one thinks he's the only one. Then one of the pimps from here took me on, I plowed for him like a Stakhanovite. Do you have any idea how many sheets I wore out before my Julian?

Pause.

My mother died. So I didn't even see her again. My aunts buried her outside of town. There's a cemetery between the kolkhoz garden and the road. We used to run out there at night when we were little. I guess it was to steal apples, though you know what kind of apples those were... Everybody's gardens were covered with them... We ran to get a good scare!

TANYA. Stephanie, But what about Mr. Julian, in seven years he still hasn't guessed that you're not a princess?

STEPHANIE. He can't tell Uzbekistan from the Baltics. For him we're all Russian bears. And nobody here reads books. In our village any peasant reads more in a winter than Julian in seven years.

TANYA. So I could become a princess, too? (*goes up to the parrot, stuffs the orange peels in his cage*).

PARROT: Get out, get out, get out, bitches!

STEPHANIE. You need more than a passport for that. You've got to learn the way I did! Well, make me some extra-strong coffee, I'm talking too much.

TANYA. Just a second, Stephanie. (*runs out*)

STEPHANIE. Here I go again... All it takes is a drink, and it starts over again. I should have my mouth sewn shut!

TANYA enters with the coffee.

TANYA. With cream, the way you like it. (*Stephanie drinks the coffee, Tanya sits at her feet*). Stephanie, I want to ask your advice. I figured out how much I'll make with you by summer... that's enough to rent a small apartment for about two months. You teach me, well, how to dress, about the forks, the ones for fruit and fish... I'll imitate you in everything. I have a nice last name, too. I'll tell everyone about how my parents were aristocracy, how my grandfathers and grandmothers were tortured in the camps!

STEPHANIE. Oh, don't make me laugh!

15

TANYA. One of the girls in my class used to talk that way, and all the guys ran after her because of it. She didn't seem anything special, but once she was an aristocrat, it seemed she was something special! I could be a prostitute. Well, what's so bad about it? My mother'll never find out! I'm not afraid of any work. I'll send my mother and daughter things, they can live half a year on one tape-recorder. And then, in two months I can find myself some Mr. Julian. Only don't be offended, Stephanie, if I leave you after the summer. Of course, you've gotten used to me, and I liked you immediately. But I'll come visit you, tell you about everything! What do you think, Stephanie, will I be able to pull it off? I'm pretty, and I have long legs.

STEPHANIE. I'm interested in what language you plan to tell them about your aristocratic blood?

TANYA. Well... I'll start with a phrase-book... at the beginning. This morning I bought bread out of the phrase-book. They understood me, yes they did.

STEPHANIE. Bring me a cigarette.

Tanya brings a cigarette, Stephanie lights up. Pause.

TANYA. Did I say anything wrong?

STEPHANIE. You amaze me, Tanya. You seem to be an adult woman, but your head's stuffed with fruit salad. How can you come to a strange country with such stuff in your head?

TANYA. Stephanie, you're offended about my leaving you by summer, aren't you?

Pause.

STEPHANIE. You'll leave, but not by summer, you'll be leaving me today.

Pause.

TANYA. (*standing up, surprised*) Today?

STEPHANIE. (*melancholically*) Un-huh.

TANYA. Where for? I don't have any place to go to.

STEPHANIE. (*blowing smoke-rings*) As they say here: that's your problem.

Pause.

TANYA. I've offended you, Stephanie, haven't I? Do you want me to beg your forgiveness.

Pause.

On my knees...

STEPHANIE. (*disgusted*) And another thing: don't ever demean yourself. Understand! You'll never make anything of yourself.

TANYA. (*crying*) But I'm not demeaning myself for my own sake! I have a mother and daughter on my hands!

STEPHANIE. That's all nonsense. Everyone has his reasons. It's just that some let others treat them like shit, others don't. You understand?

TANYA. Tell me, Stephanie, what I've done wrong.

Pause.

STEPHANIE. I'm always like this with every girl. As soon as Julian splits, I get drunk and spill my guts… And nobody should know about this.

TANYA. But I won't tell anybody! I'm good at keeping other people's secrets, you know? Everybody always confides their secrets in me…

STEPHANIE. Ouff, it's the first time I've gotten such a dunce! I don't need you once you know everything, Understand? I'm already not a Polish princess to you. Understand? You know how sick I am of eating with these frigging knives, smiling at these cretins, buying this shit and hanging it on the walls. I live holed up like a Shtirlitz.

TANYA. But am I to blame?

STEPHANIE. Don't beat up on me for pity. It's been beaten out of me. You came here on a Komsomol tour package? You don't like it here? You can register it in the complaints book.

Pause.

Bring me my purse, I've got some cash in it.

TANYA. *goes out, hanging her head.*

STEPHANIE. My God, my God!

Tanya enters, passes her the purse. Stephanie gets her wallet, counts out the money.

STEPHANIE. Here. This is what you've earned. (*Tanya takes the money*). And here's another hundred guldens for my bitchiness.

TANYA. (*take the hundred guldens*) Thank you.

STEPHANIE. Thank you? (*starts laughing*).

TANYA. (*stands a few moments in silence, then puts the hundred guldens back*) I don't need it.

STEPHANIE. (*half-rising in amazement*) Well? My congratulations! You have a chance.

Pause.

You'll get your things together. You'll slam the door. And that's it. If anything's missing… It'll cost you more. The agency warned you.

TANYA. They did.

STEPHANIE. Go. I want to be alone.

TANYA. Good-bye.

Exits. Stephanie remains lying down, smokes. Then rips herself from the bed, tosses the glass, the coffee cup, and the fruit plate into a painting. During this she wails an untranslatable Ukrainian word.

STEPHANIE. Get out! Get out! Get out! Bitches!

PARROT. (*from under the covering*) Get out! Get out! Get out! Bitches!

Stephanie savagely throws herself at the cage, pulls the parrot out like a bunch of radishes, tosses him out the window, and the cage after him.

* * *

Garden in the Shtiurm home. Yevgeny and Herbert are standing near a tree on which there is a parrot.

17

HERBERT: Where has Anita gone?

YEVGENY. She's gone to the bedroom for a book.

HERBERT: For a book? Now you're going to have a book for the whole evening, and I'll go have a whiskey. To each his own. (*In the direction of the parrot*). We've got to get a ladder and catch him.

YEVGENY. In my youth I read a lot of philosophy books, but the things that Anita introduces me to... It's just... It's just as if the world was created anew. I'll climb up the tree and try to grab him.

HERBERT: At your age there should be only one philosophy: drink, girls, and television. You'll frighten him, if you try to climb the treee.

YEVGENY. We Russians in general are very interested in philosophy. He's got to be lured somehow.

HERBERT. (*laughs*) You tell me again: Steiner said that Russia would be saved by anthroposophy! That parrot is probably worth a lot of money. I saw a lot like him when I was a soldier in Africa.

YEVGENY. Maybe Steiner was right.

HERBERT: Until that German sent you, Anita read Steiner to Bart.

YEVGENY. Who's Bart?

HERBERT: I mean our cat Bart.

YEVGENY. Your wife is a very highly spiritual woman.

HERBERT: I'll tell you a secret: I'm an old soldier, but the main soldier on Hode Bochren Street is my wife Anita. Listen, kid, anthroposophy is a plaything for the rich. Better take up business. I don't believe that you came to our country for ideas. Parrots like seeds. Go into the pantry, Anita loves to buy all kinds of junk in the natural foods store.

YEVGENY. That's true, I didn't emigrate for ideas, but anthroposophy has completely turned my view of the world upside-down.

HERBERT: You Russians are as trusting as children. It's all the same to you who you believe in: you believed Lenin, you believed Stalin, you believed Gorbachev, now you believe Yeltsin. Instead of building a house, you build an idea, you live in it and are surprised that the rain drips on you and the wind blows in.

PARROT: Get out! Get out! Get out! Bitches!

HERBERT: I can't understand what language he's yelling in. Probably his owners are coloreds. Build a house first, my boy, and then think up an idea, hang it on the wall, and admire it.

YEVGENY. You have to build a house on the idea by which the world is built. Or else it will be a bad house.

HERBERT: Listen, kid, in the bar there's a blond who'll interest you more than Steiner.

YEVGENY. I promised Anita. Maybe it likes cookies?

HERBERT: Go get some cookies. This is the first time I've seen an immigrant who wants to read books.

YEVGENY. I'm not only an immigrant. I'm a voyager. I came in search of myself.

HERBERT: Anita will like those words, but I am an old soldier, kid. I don't like it when people consider me a fool.

ANITA enters.

ANITA. Where are you going, Herbert? Why have you put on your jacket?

HERBERT: I'm going over to Nikolas's, he's bought some new stamps and wants to show them to me. I invited Yevgeny, but he claims that Steiner is more interesting for him.

ANITA. Last time you and Nikolas got so drunk you couldn't find your own house. You stopped a taxi at the Bremen's gates and demanded an explanation of why the fence had become red! Just a bit more and you would have ended up at the police station. It's shameful at your age.

HERBERT: I swear by the health of Bart, it's the last time!

ANITA. You swear by Bart's health every time. The poor cat will soon fall ill from your oaths. What's that? (*notices the parrot, puts on her glasses*).

YEVGENY. He flew in from somewhere. We're trying to figure out how to get him down.

ANITA. Oh, I know about parrots!. Everybody listen to me. Herbert, get your butterfly-net. It's in the attic. Yevgeny, get the bed-spread from the cabinet on the third floor. The green one. It has to be green. I'll lure him with a special whistle. (*Herbert and Yevgeny go out, Anita turns to the bird*). Aren't you ashamed of yourself!? You're a grown-up bird! There's a little boy or a little girl crying somewhere! They're looking for you! And you're sitting calmly in a tree and watching us with your stupid eyes! You felt like flying a bit? But they've been feeding you, cleaning your cage, taking you outside! Is this how you thank your kind owners?

Yevgeny enters with the bed-spread.

ANITA. You wave your arms to frighten him. And meanwhile Herbert will sneak up from behind with his net. And I'll whistle a special whistle. You understand?

YEVGENY. Yes, I understand.

Herbert enters.

HERBERT: The net's not there.

ANITA. You just can't be trusted to do anything! I'll go look for it myself.

HERBERT: We threw out the net five years ago.

ANITA. That can't be!

HERBERT: We threw it out when Naomi entered high school.

ANITA. How stupid. I always said: never throw anything out. The moment will come when you'll need that very thing. All right. We'll try something else. Everyone listen to me! Yevgeny will crawl up the tree with the bed-spread, and we will divert his attention to us. Only carefully, he might peck.

HERBERT: What will we do when we catch him?

ANITA. We'll place an paid advertisement in the newspaper and his happy owners will come to get him.

HERBERT: A paid advertisement for some parrot?

ANITA (*stops to think*). You're right. We'll place a free ad. And now, everybody's assembled, ready. Herbert, clap your hands and yell. I'll whistle. Yevgeny, go!

Herbert claps his hands. Yevgeny carefully climbs the tree. Anita whistles.

ANITA (*to Herbert*) Yell, yell something! Attract his attention! (*whistles*)

HERBERT. (*clapping his hands*) Right! Left! Fall in ranks! Forward! Africa is your home!

ANITA. Oh, anything but that! Yell something peaceful! This is making my blood pressure go up! (*whistles*)

HERBERT. (*clapping*) Anthroposophy will save mankind! Everyone should become an anthroposophist! Steiner, the Jesus Christ of the twentieth century!

The parrot flies up. Strictly from a production viewpoint, the parrot doesn't have to be in view! The tree he's sitting on can be higher than the visible dimensions of the stage.

YEVGENY. (*disappointed*) We frightened him! Now it'll be impossible to catch him!

ANITA. You shouldn't have yelled so loud!

HERBERT: You ordered me to yourself!

ANITA. Look, he's landed on the roof!

YEVGENY. Now we won't be able to get him down (*gets down off the tree*) Let him fly wherever he wants.

ANITA. We'll have to get a ladder.

HERBERT: That won't help, he already understands that we're trying to catch him. Look! Bart is sneaking up on him!

ANITA. We've got to chase him away!

YEVGENY. Go away! Go away! Scram! (*throws the bed-spread in the direction of the cat*)

ANITA. Away! Get away! (*Throws the Steiner volume at the cat*)

HERBERT: Bart's going to have an exotic dinner. In Africa we fried parrots with bananas. They were a little tough.

YEVGENY. Scram! Scram! Scumball!

Anita covers her face with her hands.

PARROT. (*cries his farewell*) Get out! Get out! Get out! Bitches!

Pause.

HERBERT: *Finita!* Bart's a real tiger. I think I'll go have a drink to the parrot who fell in honorable combat. (*goes off, whistling*)

Pause. Yevgeny sits on the grass, lights up a cigarette. Anita sits down beside him.

ANITA. We sent that foolish beautiful creature to his death. He might have flown and made people happy with his wondrous colors! We should have given him water and seeds. But we decided to catch him and do a good deed. We, higher creatures... That is because we are not yet anthroposophists, we are only learning to walk and to master our own spiritual reality... We destroy nature with our haste and self-confidence...

YEVGENY. It seems to me that I am like that parrot...

ANITA. Me, too, sometimes... We, weak people, must develop in ourselves the nerve, which will unite us with nature...(*gets up, takes the bed-spread, folds it*) It's gotten stained. You should have taken a different bed-spread.

YEVGENY. You said green.

ANITA. But this is light green. I'm going to take my medicine. My blood pressure has gone up. (*exits*)

YEVGENY. (*wanders around the garden, singing*). We're trav'ling, trav'ling, trav'ling, to very far-off lands. We all are peaceful neighbors, and very happy friends. Our life is very joyful, we sing a merry song, and in our song we sing about how well we get along. Tra-ta-ta, ra tat tat, we think that we shall take the cat.[1] Devil of a cat (*lies on the grass, begins to do push-ups*) One, two, three, four, five, six, seven... (*falls on the grass, lies there*)

Christopher enters. He's about sixteen years old, hair braided in pig-tails. He is wearing obscenely dirty and ripped overalls. On the bib of the overalls is scrawled "You're Fucked Up." "

CHRISTOPHER. Hi.
YEVGENY. (*getting up*) Hi.
CHRISTOPHER. Where's grannie?
YEVGENY. What grannie?
CHRISTOPHER. My grannie.
YEVGENY. (*shrugs his shoulders*) I don't understand whom you're looking for, kid?
CHRISTOPHER. I'm Christopher. Do you have any money?
YEVGENY. (*startled*) You're Herbert and Anita's grandson?
CHRISTOPHER. Yeh. Give me some money.
YEVGENY. But Christopher is in Spain...
CHRISTOPHER. That means you're in Spain, too. Give me some money.
YEVGENY. How much?
CHRISTOPHER. As much as you can.
YEVGENY. (*reaches into his pocket, gets five guldens*) Here.
CHRISTOPHER. That's not much.
YEVGENY. I haven't got much money. I've come from Russia. I'm a voyager.
CHRISTOPHER. I know. They told me. You're the Russian who's reading Steiner with grannie, in order to catch a rich anthroposophist.
YEVGENY. Who told you that?
CHRISTOPHER. The Bremens.
YEVGENY. I don't know any Bremens.
CHRISTOPHER. That's the neighbors. Their house is over there, with the red fence. That's what all of Hode Bochrem street is saying. 'Bye. (*starts to go*)
YEVGENY. Wait a minute. Where are you going?
CHRISTOPHER. I'm off.
YEVGENY. To where?
CHRISTOPHER. I'm going to Norway. No problem.
YEVGENY. Right now?
CHRISTOPHER. This evening. Now I'm going over to a girl's place.
YEVGENY. Don't you want to see your grandmother?
CHRISTOPHER. She won't give me any money.
YEVGENY. At least stop in the house. She'll be unhappy that you didn't stop in.
CHRISTOPHER. I could care less.
YEVGENY. What are you, a hippie?
CHRISTOPHER (*looks at him with pity*) I'm Christopher. No problem.

---

[1]Verses written in the 1930's by children's poet Kornei Chukovsky

YEVGENY. And how old are you?

CHRISTOPHER. Seventeen.

YEVGENY. And you always travel alone?

CHRISTOPHER. Why alone. With friends.

YEVGENY. And where are your friends?

CHRISTOPHER. I usually pick them up along the way. Now you're my friend. You gave me money, and you don't have much yourself, that means your my friend. You want to go to Norway together?

YEVGENY. What for?

CHRISTOPHER. It's beautiful there. What's that lying over there?

YEVGENY. The cat ate a parrot. A pity.

CHRISTOPHER. A pity. (*Goes up to it, picks up a feather, puts it in his hat, goes off*). 'Bye.

YEVGENY. Wait.

CHRISTOPHER. I don't have time.

Exits. Yevgeny stands in complete confusion, walks around, mechanically picking up the feathers. Anita enters.

ANITA. I spanked Bart! Probably it was unfair, but I couldn't keep my hands off him. The parrot was so sweet...

YEVGENY. But Bart isn't to blame for being a cat.

ANITA. Where's Steiner? I can't find him. I searched the whole house.

YEVGENY. You threw him at Bart. (*Goes over, picks up the book, gives it to Anita*).

ANITA. How awful! How could I? How I despise myself! (*presses Steiner to her heart*). Today I'll explain to you what Eurythmics are. You're going to have to start classes in Eurythmics. Bring two chairs out.

YEVGENY goes out.

ANITA. Poor parrot! Poor Bart! Poor Herbert! Poor Yevgeny! Poor Anita! Why is it like this? Everyone should be happy and everyone should become an anthroposophist! (*Declaims poetry, makes eurythmic motions appropriate to the text*)

Attendance prompt to orders wise
Achieves the most alluring prize;
To bring to fruit the most exalted plans
One mind is ample for a thousand hands[1].

Yevgeny enters with two chairs. They sit.

ANITA. Eurythmics is the unity of our language and our body. Man is an ideal creature and everything in him is ideal. Yesterday I showed you photographs of the works of the classics of anthroposophical sculpture, and you could convince yourself that any human bone poured in bronze or carved from marble can be aesthetic perfection and a standard of beauty. You aren't listening to me?

YEVGENY. Sorry.

---

[1]Goethe, *Faust* Part II Act V, translated by Walter Arndt, © W.W. Norton & Company, Inc., 1976, p. 292. Reprinted with permission of publisher.

ANITA. You're distressed about something?

YEVGENY. Tell me, Anita, if I had come to you without a letter of recommendation from Urse, would you still have taken me in and fed me?

ANITA. That's a hard question, Yevgeny.. And it's good that you asked it. I understand what you want say. In Amsterdam there are a lot of people who need help. If tomorrow all of them decided to become anthroposophists, then I probably would divide all my money among them. But they don't want to raise their spirituality! They don't think about the great trial that awaits them, in which only the enlightened will prevail! They only want to lie in the gutter and take narcotics...

YEVGENY. And what is your grandson Christopher doing in Spain?

ANITA. Just that. Christopher is an unfortunate child. I've not had luck with my grandchildren. Naomi is only interested in business and boys, and Christopher, only in narcotics. My daughter Elena brought them up all wrong. I demanded that they study in Waldsford school, but Elena sent them to city public schools. This is all the result of public schools and television.

YEVGENY. And aren't you worried about how he's doing in Spain?

ANITA. Let his mother worry about him. That's her problem.

YEVGENY. Does your daughter Elena work?

ANITA. Yes. She's a philosophy professor. She'll be here soon and you'll meet her. Only don't think of talking about Steiner with Elena, you'll only get unpleasant answers.

YEVGENY. Is your daughter married?

ANITA. Oh, I have a hard time understanding that. Sometimes she comes here with one, sometimes with another. Sometimes she goes to visit a third in Paris.

YEVGENY. But who is Christopher and Naomi's father?

ANITA. He's a musician. Elena always had to resolve all her problems by herself, and she left him. But they're friends, and they sometimes get together in bars and philosophize.

YEVGENY. Anita, are you happy with Herbert?

ANITA. Oh, of course! We are the most well-off family on all of Hode Bochrem street! You hear, we are the most well-off family on all of Hode Bochrem street! You hear!

YEVGENY. No.

He has a completely vacant look, he only hears along with us the rumble of train-wheels growing ever louder.

The dining-room of a little snack-bar. Tanya is washing the floor. On the counter, legs crossed, sits BADBAYAR. He is wearing a white, rather dirty robe, and a Mongolian national cap, smoking a cigar. He is about fifty.

BADBAYAR. I no like all Russian people. But Russian wash floor clean.

TANYA. I wonder what we did to you that was so bad?

BADBAYAR. Russian spoil Mongolia. Mongolia was clean, beautiful... Mountain, yurt, sheep... Russian built factory, Russian made communism, Russian force children boarding-school... Children live Yurt, drink kumiss, sing song, was good... Russian take children boarding-school... Make up disease... Russian teach to steal...

TANYA. That's enough, I'm sure that there wasn't anything good about your yurt.

BADBAYAR. Yurt need nothing... Sheep, sun, horse...

TANYA. Well, but if someone in your yurt got sick, you didn't even have a telephone to call a doctor.

BADBAYAR. In Yurt Mongol not sick: fresh air, fresh meat, heal with herbs. Mine sister Ayuna poor, live yurt, gallop horse, always healthy... I live Amsterdam, many guldens, always sick!

TANYA. Then why don't you go back?

BADBAYAR. Badbayar used to refrigerator, Badbayar used to whiskey, Badbayar used to Europe. At night sleep, see Mongolia, see sun, see steppe, see Mongolian girl... You see Terel'zh? You see Molost? You see Chingyl'? You see nothing!

TANYA. (*washing the floor*) I don't miss it at all. I don't have time. Only I miss my daughter and I miss my mother a little... sometimes I think, what if one of them got sick, and I'm here.

BADBAYAR. Amsterdam women no pretty. Big, coarse, smell of soap. Mongol women tender, smell of milk...

TANYA. I'm not pretty either?

BADBAYAR. No pretty.

TANYA. (*stops from unexpectedness*) Then why do you sleep with me?

BADBAYAR. No need pay guldens.

TANYA. And if I reject you? Say no, and that's it!

BADBAYAR. You no find other work.

TANYA. And if I do?

BADBAYAR. No find! I Amsterdam am live ten years. Escape China, sail Holland. You no find other work. You come Badbayar, Badbayar give less guldens for same work.

Tanya wrings out the rag, barely can keep herself from bumping into Badbayar.

BADBAYAR. Why you so high strung? I no like high strung. I like kind.

TANYA. Maybe a millionaire will fall in love with me and marry me! Then I'll have your place shut down!

BADBAYAR. Millionaire no come to Badbayar, Come here poor, dirty. Millionaire go other restaurant!

TANYA. Then I'll clean up everything, get dressed, and go for a walk in the streets! And I'll meet someone.

BADBAYAR. You meet bandit. Tanya evening tired. Tired woman like bee without honey. Rich man no meet tired girl (*jumps up from seat, without taking the cigar out of his mouth, starts to lift up her skirt from behind*).

TANYA. (*face distorted from repulsion*) Don't touch me! I haven't finished washing the floor!

BADBAYAR. You finish after.

TANYA. I can't today! I can't today! Understand?

BADBAYAR. Then you can't, yesterday you can't, always can't! Guldens you can, Badbayar can't!

TANYA. Well, Badbayardchik, sweetie, tomorrow! Yes, honest, tomorrow!

BADBAYAR. Floor washed, dishes washed, potatoes peeled.

TANYA. (*in horror*) But there's a whole kettleful of potatoes! I'm keeling over from fatigue! Barbara should be peeling the potatoes!

BADBAYAR. Tanya peel potatoes. Badbayar can have Barbara, Barbara no peel potatoes. Badbayar cannot have Tanya, Tanya peel potatoes. Badbayar is master. (*goes to the door, puffing importantly on his cigar*).

TANYA. I want to eat!

Badbayar stops, turns to the counter, bends over, gets a covered dish with fried potatoes and fish.

BADBAYAR. Fish. Eat.

Tanya takes a chair, puts it near the pail and rags, takes the dish on her knees, looks at her hands, begins eating.

TANYA. It's cold.

BADBAYAR. Say: thank you.

TANYA. Thank you.

BADBAYAR. Say it in Mongolian! I taught you. You talking to Mongol.

TANYA. Bayrala.

BADBAYAR. Correct.

TANYA. You feed me with leftovers off the customers' plates.

BADBAYAR. Tanya greedy! Hides her guldens, eats what others not eat.

Tanya eats in silence. Badbayar goes up to her, pulls a fish out of the dish by its tail.

TANYA. But there are only three fish here!

BADBAYAR. Badbayar no eat fish. Mongol no eat fish. Cat eat fish. Cat have no guldens.

Triumphantly walks with cigar in one hand, fish in the other.

TANYA. Bastard! Slitty-eyed bastard! I'd like to take an automatic rifle to you!

Finishes eating, puts the dish on the table, wipes her hands on her skirt, takes out of her pocket a notebook and pen.

TANYA. (*writes, speaking the words aloud*) My dearest ones, Mama and Sonechka! Everything here is fine. At first I worked for a rich immigrant woman. She was like a mother to me. Then I left her, because I found work in an elegant restaurant. The work isn't hard, The owner is a Mongol. He is very kind. He's fifty years old. He doesn't have any family, so he treats me like a daughter. The people here are very nice, everyone smiles at each other in the streets, but they are completely different from our people. And I haven't gotten used to it. How's Sonechka's music? How are you all? I bought Sonechka a jacket, the sleeves are a little long, so it will last for two years. It will outlive all of us! I'm also sending some videocassettes; give them to Vadik, he'll sell them and give you the money. Much love. My heart doesn't bother me at all here. Your Tanya (*cries*).

A bedroom in the Shtrium house. Morning. Yevgeny sits on the windowsill wearing headphones, listening to music, looking out the window.

ELENA. (*raises herself out of bed, stares at him a long time, smiles*) Good morning!

Yevgeny doesn't hear her.

25

ELENA. (*louder*) Good morning!

Yevgeny still doesn't hear.

Elena takes a piece of clothing that was hastily thrown on the floor the night before, and throws it at him.

YEVGENY. (*turns, takes off the ear-phones*) Excuse me. (*By his facial expression, it can be seen that he feels lousy*)
ELENA. Good morning.

Pause.

ELENA. Still couldn't figure out yesterday, have they hired you as a gardener?

Pause.

YEVGENY. I haven't figured it out myself.
ELENA. How much do they pay you per day?
YEVGENY. They don't pay me.
ELENA. Then what are you doing here?

Pause.

YEVGENY. I don't know. I drink with Herbert. I go with Anita to the anthroposophic society and to Eurythmics. As of yesterday, I ended up in bed with you. Maybe that's what's called a gardener. Maybe something else... I don't know.
ELENA. Kid, I see you have big problems.
YEVGENY. No problem, as your son Christopher says.
ELENA. How do you know what my son says?
YEVGENY. He was here.
ELENA. Why didn't my parents say anything about it?
YEVGENY. He spoke with me for a little while and then left. He didn't want to meet them.
ELENA. And where is he now?
YEVGENY. He said he was going to Norway.
ELENA. To Norway? Norway's beautiful. Christopher's a delight!
YEVGENY. I should have left with him.
ELENA. How old are you?
YEVGENY. Thirty-three.
ELENA. Then you're exactly seventeen years too late. Come over here.
  Yevgeny goes over to her, sits down, they embrace.
ELENA. There's winter in your face.
YEVGENY. I feel very good with you. I feel bad by myself.
ELENA. We had too much to drink yesterday. You're feeling bad from that.
YEVGENY. I came to the West to make a lot of money, so that one day I could return and drive past my ex-wife in a Mercedes, to see her stupid face contort at the sight! Understand?
ELENA. Do Russians always pour out their souls so quickly?
YEVGENY. (*angrily*) Always!
ELENA. But that's so imprudent, we've known each other only one night.

YEVGENY. (*yells*) I don't care! For the sake of clouding the face of a woman I always held in contempt, for three years I have been doing things to myself that my worst enemy wouldn't do! I've sunk to bottom! I almost became a thief! Understand?

ELENA. (*stroking his head*)   Everything will be all right, calm down... We should have a drink.

YEVGENY. I almost robbed a little idiot who came here the same way I did. I came into your parents' house with a forged letter. I didn't even know who Steiner was. That's the same way I went to take exams at the institute... It was a kind of sport, to see if I could put one over on the professor or not. I really wanted to work my way into some meditating do-nothing's guldens, and believe me, I would make her happier than Steiner. And now, something has snapped in me.

ELENA. Why are you telling me all this?

YEVGENY. Because you're the first person in three years here who can understand what I'm talking about. All the rest have a sign written on their faces: "That's your problem, kid."

ELENA. But it really is your problem. Your arrogance has made a slave of you, and you yell so loud, as if the whole world were to blame. It seemed to me that I'm also guilty in you eyes.

YEVGENY. It's not my arrogance, it's my country that made me a slave.

ELENA. I don't believe that there exists a country in which there are only slaves. Even under slave-ownership, some were slaves by circumstance, others by consciousness.

YEVGENY. So in your opinion I'm to blame myself?

ELENA. An intelligent person is always to blame himself, a stupid person is guilty in believing an evil one.

YEVGENY. I don't know what else to do, Elena...

Pause.

ELENA. But I know... First I'll kiss you, and then... when we're both tired, we'll drink coffee with cream, a little champagne, go into the garden, and then we'll discuss everything seriously and calmly. Okay?

YEVGENY. Okay! (*Kisses her*).

They embrace. A knock at the door.

ELENA. What happened?

ANITA'S VOICE. Open up!

ELENA. I'm sleeping.

ANITA'S VOICE. Open up immediately!

ELENA. What is this? An atomic war? A meteor shower? Or maybe the appearance of the Antichrist and only those who have read Steiner will be saved? I'm sleeping.

Anita bangs the door with her fists.

ANITA'S VOICE. I demand that you open up immediately!

ELENA. And I demand that you not keep me from sleeping!

ANITA'S VOICE. Where's Yevgeny?

ELENA. How should I know?

ANITA'S VOICE. Because he's in your room.

ELENA. It's your imagination.

ANITA'S VOICE. Open up immediately! I heard his voice through the door.

ELENA. (*to Yevgeny*) Oh, now there'll be a real storm! Get dressed.

They jump up from the bed and dressed hurriedly, fumbling with their jeans and tee-shirts.

YEVGENY: You put on my jeans.

ELENA. It doesn't matter now.

Elena opens the door. Anita enters, in a robe thrown over her pajamas. She walks to the other side of the room, sits on the edge of a chair. She is beside herself.

ANITA. Listen, Elena, this exceeds all bounds!

ELENA. Good morning, Mama!

ANITA. How old are you, Elena?

ELENA. If I'm not mistaken, Mama, you gave birth to me forty-two years ago!

ANITA. This boy is young enough to be your son!

ELENA. You never were very good at math, Mama!

ANITA. I was silent when you seduced the Bremen's boy!!

ELENA. That "boy" was greying at the temples, Mama!

ANITA. I was silent when you were the lover of old Marta's warden! That bull with a pistol!

ELENA. Mama, before becoming a bull with a pistol, he was a professor of theoretical physics!

ANITA. You even had an affair with Willie the terrorist!

ELENA. Being a terrorist is work, too. He didn't have anything to feed his children with!

ANITA (*jumps up and yells*) Will you ever stop interrupting me?! What did you need Yevgeny for? He's a pure boy, whose soul is full of Russian longing and belief in the light! You stole my children from me! You filled their heads with your idiotic freedom! Your freedom is freedom from everything! From goodness, from principles, from responsibility! All Hode Bochrem street shudders when your automobile enters it! What do you want from Yevgeny?

YEVGENY. Anita, My respect for you knows no bounds, but you shouldn't insult Elena.

ANITA. I know my daughter! She's capable of corrupting an angel! How I hate her for this!

ELENA. That's it. I'm leaving.

YEVGENY. Me, too.

ANITA. You stay!

YEVGENY. This is impossible. You have been very kind to me, but it's no longer possible...

ANITA. Today we have a class... in Eurythmics.

YEVGENY. Anita, forgive me. I have to tell you.

Pause.

The letter from Urse was a forgery.

Pause.

28

ANITA. I knew that right away. The letter isn't the issue...
YEVGENY. Right away?... Forgive me... (*runs out*)
ELENA. My greetings. (*takes her bag, goes out*).
ANITA (*yells*) Slut!

Paces around the room, tries to calm down.

ANITA. I hate even numbers! On even-numbered days something always happens. On the second Bart swallowed a parrot, on the tenth my pie burned, today Elena's taken that boy away! (*yells through the open door*). Herbert! Herbert! How long can one sleep! Call the agency, have them plant all the while roses from the greenhouse in the garden! I can't stand this any longer!

* * *

A small train station. Tanya is seated on a bench, wrapped up in a plaid blanket, next to her are two suitcases. She is shelling an egg, throws the shell in an urn. Near her on the bench sleeps long-legged, long-haired MARTIN. Martin has a tender feminine face, a thin voice, and a big ring in his ear. He has a multicolored unisex suit. A musical chord from the station loud-speaker and announcement awaken Martin. He opens his eyes, stretches, sits up, and looks at Tanya joyfully.

MARTIN. Hi, there.
TANYA. Hi.
MARTIN. Do you want to eat?
TANYA. (*in English*) Excuse me, I speak English badly.
MARTIN. Are you hungry? (*points at her egg*)
TANYA. (*deciding that he's asking for her egg, hastily sticks it in her mouth, choking*) Excuse me, my English very bad. I don't understand you.
MARTIN.(*looking at her with pity*). Let's go have breakfast in the restaurant. I'm inviting you. Be my guest. (*Puts his hand to his heart*)
TANYA. (*supposing that he's asking her for an egg, the difficult struggle is reflected in her face, she reaches in her purse, gets out a hard-boiled egg, peels it into the urn, offers it to Martin*). Be my guest.
MARTIN.(*at first is stunned, then laughs, seeing that Tanya is offended, takes the egg and begins to eat*). Thank you. You're very kind. Thank you.
TANYA. What's your name?
MARTIN. Martin.
TANYA. Martina?
MARTIN. My name is Martin.
TANYA. My name is Tanya. Are you a man or a woman?
MARTIN.(*smiling*) The government considers me a man, people consider me a woman, and I consider myself a bird. Understand?

TANYA. I don't understand. I speak English very badly. (*she takes out a dictionary, looks up a word*) I'm Russian. From Russia. I don't have work. I have no place to sleep. I have fear of police. I have no friends in Amsterdam. I have in Russian little daughter and old mother. Understand? I need work! I need a lot of money! Understand?

MARTIN. May I help you?

TANYA. I don't know...

MARTIN. I'm a theater director.

TANYA. Manager?

MARTIN. Director. It's a very special theater. It's very small. I do social sculpture. Understand?

TANYA. I don't understand. I'm looking for work.

MARTIN. You understand, humans have polluted the world, and for that the world has polluted humanity. The world can be saved only through the cleansing of humanity. A cleansed person can begin to cleanse the world. You understand, you have to go out into the streets and begin to wash and clean. This is my conception of the salvation of mankind. The only real prayer today is a clean scrap of earth. You understand?

TANYA. I understand English very badly.

MARTIN. You have to understand! You have such a wonderful face! You have a face like a bouquet of wildflowers!

TANYA. I have very bad, very little English.

MARTIN. How can I explain it to you? I'm proposing work to you. Work! You understand?

TANYA. Work? I understand.

MARTIN. You will be an actress in my theater.

TANYA. Work? How many guldens? I'm looking for work!

MARTIN.(*gestures*) You will wash, clean, floors, walls, pavement, you will wipe the leaves on the trees.

TANYA. (*in horror*) Wash? Wash again? I don't want to wash anymore!

MARTIN. This is a dialogue with the universe, understand? One day all people will go out into the street and wash the whole world clean in one day. You understand?

TANYA. I don't understand. I'm ready to do any work. How many guldens?

MARTIN. Holland is a very clean country, they should grasp my ideas very quickly.

TANYA. (*at the end of her rope*) How many guldens?

MARTIN. Why are you only talking about money? Is that the only thing you need?

TANYA. I don't understand so fast. How many guldens for one hour. I can work a lot.

MARTIN. Listen, I have a lot of money, but I'm very unhappy. I have seen many poor but happy people. Money is the first way men polluted the world. Can it really be that you only need money. Only money?

TANYA. I only need money. I also need one person... a man. He's Russian. He's in Amsterdam. I don't know his name. Help me. Help me, please.

MARTIN.(*embraces her*) I'll help you. We'll find him.

* * *

Kitchen in Elena's house. Elena is grating an apple on a grater. She has a terry-cloth robe on. Yevgeny is pacing around and smoking. He has on a similar robe.

ELENA. You want some coffee?
YEVGENY. No.
ELENA. You want some champagne?
YEVGENY. No.

Pause.

YEVGENY. You mean you're really going to abandon everything and go to Cologne?
ELENA. Yes.
YEVGENY. You mean you'll really drive to Cologne just because this German phoned you?
ELENA. I'm not abandoning anything. I don't have any classes for a month.
YEVGENY. What about me?
ELENA. You can live here.
YEVGENY. On your money?
ELENA. I gave you a letter of introduction to my friends. They're looking for a Russian translator. You can live on your own money.
YEVGENY. You mean all this month I was your boy for intimate services. Is that it?
ELENA. In my opinion, that which you call intimate services was mutual.
YEVGENY. But I lived on your money.
ELENA. What's the difference... (*massages the peeled apple onto her face and neck*).
YEVGENY. What are you doing?
ELENA. It's a skin treatment.
YEVGENY. You mean that for a fifty-year-old German whom you met once in your life and who called you after a year, you need an apple, and for me you were just fine without it?
ELENA. He called when he understood that he really needs me. We agreed to call each other only if that happened. As a matter of fact, a year isn't that much time.

Pause.

YEVGENY. I only understand one thing, that Anita was right! You really are a slut! In that mask you look like a scarecrow!
ELENA. (*coldly*) But I'm not always going to be in this mask. I'll wash it off!
YEVGENY. Now I understand why your son Christopher is a drug-addict and your daughter Naomi's only concern is boys!
ELENA. All young people experience drugs and sex, that's normal. I passed through that stage myself. Everything's going to be all right with my children, they're just on the road to selfhood. (*turns on the tape-recorder, starts to dance*).
YEVGENY. You are a hundred times more shameless than a Russian woman!
ELENA. Why?

31

YEVGENY. Because any Russian woman would find some lie for why she was going to Cologne.

ELENA. Why lie?

YEVGENY. But you don't need him.

ELENA. I don't know. We saw each other once. We spoke for several hours in a bar. That was in Peking. We sat by a fountain and spoke Italian, so that his friends wouldn't understand us. There was a dictionary lying on the table that we passed between us. We drew pictures on napkins and hid them in our pockets. Sometimes we completely misunderstood each other, sometimes we understood each other as no one ever had before. Germans have an expression: to speak along one's heart-line. I had to fly home. I decided not to change my ticket.

YEVGENY. Probably he's some superman.

ELENA. (*laughs*) He stoops a little, he's a wall-flower in funny glasses. He has amazing eyes and fingers smudged with paint.

YEVGENY. What kind of paint?

ELENA. Blue. He's an artist. He was painting a mural in Peking. He had the crazy idea of painting murals on all the white walls in the world. I think he needs me.

YEVGENY. I don't understand how Herbert and Anita could have raised such a cynical daughter.

ELENA. My dear, I grew up in the most well-off family on all of Hode Bochrem street! My father fought in Africa, he thought that would make a real man of him. It made him a vulgar burgher. My mother all her life hated my father for marrying her for her money, and me for not breaking with him. In her old age she has found comfort in anthroposophy and hates everyone who lives more freely than she does.

YEVGENY. But I need you!

ELENA. I can't make you happy. We have different levels of internal freedom. In your model of love there are two slaves, in mine, two masters. We speak different languages. You enter the space of my freedom and you try to make it into a dictatorship of love.

YEVGENY. All right, I agree to any conditions.

ELENA. The word "conditions" abbrogates the word "agreement." Relations between men and women should be like a dance in which you sometimes come near, sometimes go apart, but you are bound to your partner by a multitude of elastic threads, which stretch into space and do not rip apart. When both feel each other, but remain themselves at the same time.

Pause.

YEVGENY. What's his name?

ELENA. Wilfried.

YEVGENY. (*runs out of the kitchen, returns with a suitcase, and begins to throw things around*). Is this the dress you wanted to meet him in? (*rips the dress in half*).

She turns off the music, sits down and observes him coldly.

YEVGENY. Or maybe this one? (*He rips another dress, throws all the rest around, goes over to the window, turns away*).

She carefully lifts a wallet he had thrown out of the suitcase, hides it under her robe near her chest. Pause.

ELENA. You have to calm down.
YEVGENY. Forgive me. My nerves just gave out.
ELENA. I didn't think you would be so upset.

Pause.

We still have two hours.
YEVGENY. And what are we going to do?
ELENA. (*smiles*) First I'll kiss you, then... when we're tired, we'll drink some coffee with cream, then a little champagne, then go into the garden and talk about everything seriously and calmly.

He turns around, makes a step toward her. She withdraws.

ELENA. First I'll take a shower. You said that I looked like a scarecrow in this mask. And turn the music up louder, I want to be able to hear it in the bathroom.

Yevgeny turns on the music, begins to dance, waving the ripped dresses. Then he sits on the floor, lights up a cigarette. Turns off the music, then jumps up, runs to the window, freezes, and with a thunderstruck expression, walks back.

YEVGENY. She left... She got in the car right in her robe and left for Cologne. She didn't even wipe the apple off her face.

Walks around the room, mechanically folding things into the suitcase. Pours some whiskey, drinks, sits on the windowsill. The telephone rings. Yevgeny doesn't react for a long time, then picks up the receiver nonetheless.

YEVGENY. Hello. I'm listening. Elena left. For Cologne. This is Yevgeny. Who? Christopher? It's you? You're calling from Norway? Is it beautiful there? You know, Christopher, I'm feeling really bad... Help me? You're too far away, kid. You'll come here because of me? In the morning? (*puts down the receiver*). He's coming in the morning... That's impossible... He said: No problem.

* * *

Basement in which Martin's group is rehearsing. Jacqueline is sitting on the floor and combing her long hair. Richard is playing his trumpet. Martin is sitting next to Tanya, who is dressed in black tights. Strewn on the floor are brushes, rags, sponges, brooms, and some bright plastic buckets of water.

MARTIN. You have to concentrate. You have to pull yourself together, as if for a prayer. You understand? Don't you?
TANYA. (*confused*) I'm supposed to wash the floor, right?
JACQUELINE: It was a mistake bringing her here. You won't get anything out of her. We need a professional actress.
MARTIN.(*to Tanya*) I am a tree. You are to wash my branches and leaves (*stretches out his hand to her*) You understand?

TANYA. (*nods*) I understand. (*takes a sponge, dampens it in the bucket, wrings it out, with concentration washes Martin's hand*).

JACQUELINE: Her eyes are empty. She isn't an actress, she's a charwoman.

MARTIN. You must do this with love. You understand? Love! Love! You must love the tree when you wash it. Understand?

TANYA. I don't understand.

MARTIN. Look. Jacqueline, come over here. (*Jacqueline approaches, sticks her hand forward with the comb*) . This is a tree, see how I am going to wash it. (*takes the sponge out of Tanya's hand, carefully and gently washes the comb in Jacqueline's hands, then, rolling up the sleeve of her dress, washes her hand*). In my every touch there should be love. You understand?

TANYA. I don't understand. Forgive me, I don't understand.

MARTIN.sinks to the floor, fatigued.

RICHARD: She's from Russia. I've been told that everything is different there. Try to explain to her in some other way.

JACQUELINE: We have to perform tomorrow. We'll have to look for someone else.

MARTIN. Our translator should have been here an hour ago. I don't want another actress. I like her face, her body. In these Russians there's some kind of morbid passion. You just have to find the key to it.

JACQUELINE: You'll be looking for the key to her for a hundred years. Call the actor's guild, they'll send you an unemployed actress.

MARTIN. She has big problems. A person with problems is always more interesting than a professional actor. She's interesting to watch. It's impossible to take your eyes off her.

JACQUELINE: You've simply fallen in love with this Russian woman!

RICHARD: I've been told that they have nothing to eat there, like in Africa. Only bananas. She can't understand why she should wash a tree when there isn't anything to eat. (*continues playing his trumpet*).

MARTIN. Tanya, let's try again.

Tanya obediently approaches. Martin takes her by the hand and leads her to the edge of the stage.

MARTIN. Look, there's the sun. It loves us. And this is grass, it lets us step on it. Take off your shoes. (*they both take off their shoes*). You feel how the grass loves you. Do you understand me?

TANYA. Yes.

MARTIN. And this is the wall of a house that shelters us against the cold. Go up to it, wash it. You understand?

TANYA. Yes. (*She takes the sponge and begins to wash the wall, gradually descending into the auditorium, she doesn't notice anyone, her face is beaming*).

MARTIN. Look at her! Look at her face! She understands everything!

JACQUELINE: Very good!

RICHARD: You were right, Martin... (*plays the trumpet*).

YEVGENY. (*enters*). *No one pays any attention to him.*

YEVGENY. (*he is very glum*) Hello. I'm late, forgive me. An extreme situation. I speak German and French as fluently as English. My name is Yevgeny. Here is my letter of recommendation from Elena Shtrium.

MARTIN.(*turning to him*) Quiet! Look how our new actress is working. She understood everything without a translator! I am glad that you came anyway... Just look at her... She's working along the heart-line.

Yevgeny sees Tanya.

MARTIN.(*to Tanya*) You will wash this wall, then you will wash the other wall. Gradually we will wash the whole world! Then artists will come and cover these walls with paint. Then there will come free and patient people who will not say to each other: you will do this my way! They will have children who won't need to search for themselves because in freedom people are born complete selves!

STEPHANIE enters.

MARTIN. Who are you?

STEPHANIE. I lost my parrot, I want to wash something.

MARTIN.(*gives her a bucket and sponge*). Be my guest. (*Stephanie washes*).

HERBERT enters.

HERBERT. I am very lonely... I would like to wash something.

JACQUELINE (*gives him a bucket and sponge*) Be my guest.

ANITA enters.

ANITA. It's been so long since I've seen my grand-children. I <u>must</u> wash something.

RICHARD (*Gives her a bucket and sponge*). Be my guest.

CHRISTOPHER enters.

CHRISTOPHER. I'm ready to wash something. No problem.

TANYA. (*gives him a bucket and sponge*). Be my guest.

ELENA. enters.

ELENA. I still have two hours. I can wash something, too.

YEVGENY. (*gives her a bucket and sponge*) Be my guest.

BADBAYAR enters.

BADBAYAR. Mongolia clean. Europe dirty. I want to wash.

MARTIN. (*Gives him a bucket and sponge*). Be my guest.

They wash the floors and walls, involving the spectators in the process, then go out of the theater building, wash the streets, wash the city, they wash the whole world...

Elena Gremina posing as Catherine the Great signing legislation "On the Liberty of the Gentry" on the set of *Behind the Mirror* in Youngstown, Ohio, May 1995.

Elena Gremina

BEHIND THE MIRROR

A Play in Two Parts

Dramatis Personae

MATUSHKA ("Little Mother")
SASHENKA
LADY COUNTESS BRUCE

BEHIND THE MIRROR
A play in two parts

The action takes place in Russia, in Saint Petersburg, in 1779-1784.

"The years passed, her power continued to grow, Her desires became more and more unbridled: Her favorites of the last years didn't dare leave the palace without her permission, even to come out without authorization from the special place, which was separated from her formal bedroom by a screen in the form of a mirror. According to her wishes the mirror could be lifted up at any moment. When the mirror was down, several of the foreign guests expressed curiosity about the purpose of the room behind the divider, Catherine would invariably answer that there was a chamber-pot."

—From an eighteenth-century anecdote of Russian court life.

PART I
Scene One

A mirrored hall lighted by many candles in candelabras. COUNTESS BRUCE, dressed in mourning, covers the mirrors with black gauze.

LADY BRUCE. The drama of ill-fated youth, vain love, and the triumph of treachery. Rumors and conjectures.

Looks around. And moves toward the goal which has long enticed her: in the corner is a simple working desk, on its green cloth are placed a writing-set, an inked quill pen, a sheet of good expensive paper dusted with sand - a letter that was begun, but not finished... BRUCE reads at first to herself, then mumbles aloud, repeats phrases, squinting her eyes, as if repeating a lesson that has been assigned her.

Mein Liebe Freund. My dear and learned friend. When I began this letter, I was happy and gay. My thoughts flew so fast, that I did not know how it would end. Now it's all changed! I am killed by grief! My happiness is no more! My best friend has died. I had hoped that he would be the support of my old age; He was accommodating himself to that, he used every opportunity to acquire my tastes. This was a youth whom I had cultivated, who was noble, tender, and grateful; he shared with me my troubles, when I had them, and took joy in my joys! In a word, as I weep, I have the misfortune to tell you that General Lanskoi is no more!

BRUCE bursts into laughter, whirls around the room, spreading her skirts, carefully lays the letter on its previous place and dusts it with powder again.

Mein Liebling, only to your enlightened sympathies can I confess that my very room, that used to be so pleasant, has turned into an empty cave, which I move around with difficulty, like a shadow... Was it so long ago—mein Gnedige Freund—that I wrote you of the intoxicating bliss of our first meeting?!..

Moves away from the desk Takes a feather-duster, brushes away the dust...

Scene Two

...Tripping, SASHENKA appears. He is in white tights and a green uniform, holds a three-corned hat awkwardly under his arm.

SASHENKA. (*gazing around*). Here I am... I'm done for, done for...

BRUCE. (*coldly*). Who's there?

They look at each other.

SASHENKA. Uh... Lieutenant Alexander Dmitrievich Lanskoi... I was summoned to appear.. ordered... (*Gets tongue-tied*)

BRUCE. And what of it?

SASHENKA. (*in a fallen voice*)   Their Excellency's command... Their Royal Highness... According to Their personal command... To appear and fulfill Their every...

BRUCE. (*shortly*). Ah.

Looks Sashenka over with renewed interest.

SASHENKA. At your complete disposal, since otherwise... (*Becomes completely confused under Bruce's gaze*). And what about me? Papa's dead, and Their Highness—serve your Fatherland...

A long pause. BRUCE walks around him with tiny steps, studying him like a statue. Then guffaws until she falls on the bed.

BRUCE. This is really something! The last one was Pyrrhus, the Epirian king, but this one... Well, Your Highness! (*And a new fit of laughter*).

SASHENKA. (*worried*). None of this is clear to me.

BRUCE. (*laughing*). Not clear! It's not clear to him! Here the best minds... His Highness himself...

SASHENKA. (*haltingly*). Permit me to say... I am at the complete disposal of Lady Countess Bruce... at the complete disposal, there is no other way to say it.

Pause.

BRUCE. (*coldly, in a businesslike manner*). Matushka is to be called —Aurora.

SASHENKA. (*whispers*). Aurora. (*Horrified.*) How so?

BRUCE. Aurora. That's what she likes. They all have called her that. That's how it's to be.

Pause.

In the desk, in a little pink box - are gold coins, a hundred thousand. This is for the beginning. Later—there will be more, depending on your service. His Highness was given an entire million the first morning.

SASHENKA. Holy Lord God, save and have mercy upon me.

BRUCE. Matushka is extremely demanding. She has been loved by bogatyrs.

SASHENKA. (*sadly*). Everybody knows that.

BRUCE. Matushka loves quick-wittedness and brilliant answers.

Pause.

There's nothing to be done about it. His Highness has already talked about you, there's nothing to be done about it.

Pause.

There's the mirror. There's the hall, the formal bedroom. The mirror sometimes comes down, sometimes goes up, there's a special mechanism. Now there's a Swedish emissary and the reception for the East Prussian Deputies. It is very important for the entire fate of the Fatherland—is there to be a new war. His Highness is also there.

SASHENKA. And I?

BRUCE. When they all leave, the mirror will rise. When Matushka decides to relax. She often likes to relax in the middle of the day.

SASHENKA. (*horrified*). In the middle of the day, too?

BRUCE. In the middle of the day, too. Everything about Matushka is unusual. Her organism is not like that of other mortals. You have certainly heard—rumors and conjectures?

SASHENKA. Can all that really be true?

BRUCE. (*triumphantly*). Matushka arises at five in the morning. Matushka has two ears—left and right—they hear independently of one another, which is why Matushka doesn't like any music and doesn't understand why others are enthralled. Matushka even injected herself with smallpox vaccine.

SASHENKA. Can it really be that everything, everything they say is true?

BRUCE. Her scarf, her foulard, Matushka wraps around her head for the night. Then during the day sparks fly from it. The chambermaid, the Kalmyk girl Katerina Ivanovna, told me about it.

SASHENKA. (*hopefully*). Everything, everything that they say about her—that's not possible.

BRUCE shakes the scarf. It crackles and sparks fly.

BRUCE. This is the scarf from Matushka's head. It's from her nighttime thoughts.

SASHENKA. (*after a pause*). Don't seek to serve, but don't refuse to serve. That's what Papa used to tell me. Not long before his sudden death.

Noise and creaking.

BRUCE. The mirror! It's the mirror! The mirror is about to rise. Now we shall behold Matushka with our own eyes.

SASHENKA. (*covering himself with crosses*). Don't refuse to serve. That's what Papa would say. Right before his sudden death. Don't refuse to serve.

And here the mirror rises.

The second half of the bed, which previously was hidden by the mirror, is seen. And on this bed sits a respectable-looking woman of middle age, in a ruffled cap and glasses, flipping through some manuscript,

This is MATUSHKA.

MATUSHKA. (*with a thick German accent*). Phooey, Phooey! What lousy work! What in the world am I to do if there's a new person appointed to a new position and again does lousy work! The work must be good, always good. Work that is consistently good is the condition of happiness.

BRUCE. (*curtseys*). Matushka...

MATUSHKA. My dear heart, my friend! What am I to do? They complain to me of persecution and abuse. I dismiss from office. It's a dishonor for the whole fatherland, when my dignitaries are called such names!

BRUCE. Matushka, this is Alexander Dmitrievich Lanskoi. His Highness spoke of him to you.

MATUSHKA. (*looks Sashenka over, he freezes*). Grigory's a grifter. Eh? What do you think? Igor is over-eager. Oh, I know too much.

BRUCE. Young man, don't stand there like a pillar of salt. Let Matushka look you over.

MATUSHKA. And so I dismiss him from his post, make new appointments. But no! Once again thefts from the treasury and abuses. New people, young people, and they're already corrupted. I feel lost. I write to my friends—Diderot, Voltaire. They answer with general arguments about human nature. This is all very fine, gentlemen! But how is it that a new young man, appointed by me personally, has stolen in three months as much as his predecessor did in five years! What is this? Is he afraid he won't be able to manage otherwise?

BRUCE. His Highness recommended highly the services of Lieutenant Lanskoi.

MATUSHKA. I don't know what to do. The East Prussian delegation...

BRUCE. (*interrupts her*). Lieutenant Lanskoi, at your service. Ready to serve. With all the fervor of youth. A young man of twenty-two...

MATUSHKA. (*absentmindedly*). That's nice.

SASHENKA. Twenty-four!

BRUCE. He looks younger, doesn't he? Height, over five feet ten inches...

SASHENKA. I... I didn't tell you! How did you know?

BRUCE. Oh, it's obvious now!

SASHENKA. Nine! Nine inches, not ten!

BRUCE. Excellent health. Was examined by Doctor Rodgerson.

MATUSHKA. (*takes off her glasses, looks at Sashenka attentively*). Vaccinated against smallpox?

SASHENKA. (*in horror, yells*). NO!

MATUSHKA. (*graciously*). Oh, that's easily corrected. We'll think about it. Young man...

BRUCE. Alexander Dmitrievich!

MATUSHKA. ...Alexander Dmitrievich, His Highness the Prince spoke to me about you and about your feelings. Is it all true?

SASHENKA. (*disconnectedly*). Papa... Papa... before his cruel, sudden death... From service, he said... you shouldn't...

BRUCE. Everything, everything is true. The purest truth.

Sashenka faints.

Scene Three

Bruce, Matushka alone. Silence.

MATUSHKA. How pleasant, when such a young man is capable of such feeling.

BRUCE. His Highness himself attested to that.

MATUSHKA. (*absent-mindedly, thinking about something else.*) The East Prussian deputation! What am I to do with the East Prussian deputation! His Highness once again contradicted me.

Pause.

My one joy—I am surrounded by friends. Surrounded by devotion.

BRUCE. Matushka.

MATUSHKA. You mustn't. Don't tell me anything.

BRUCE curtseys.

One thing, one thing alone disheartens me. He doesn't understand—His Highness the Prince. He doesn't understand that he is putting himself in a ridiculous position. A worthless creature! And is she really so very pretty?

BRUCE spreads her arms in a gesture of indecision.

Tell me—you, you of all people always tell the truth—can it be that she is as pretty as they say?

Pause.

But if she really is so pretty—it's ridiculous, just like his opinion about the East Prussian question. And everyone is making fun of it. They speak aloud, whisper loudly. They say, the point of concern isn't the East Prussian question; it's a cute little face. And her husband's Livonian lands.

BRUCE. They say he adores her.

MATUSHKA. I don't understand such women. Everyone adores them—deceived husbands, generous lovers. Everyone adores them, and without any effort on their part. Explain it to me.

BRUCE. (*sadly*). I don't understand, either.

Pause.

Matushka!

MATUSHKA. Don't talk about anything.

Pause.

How is that young man? How is he feeling?

Pause.

Let's go find out. We have to think about what to call him.

BRUCE. (*flatteringly*). He resembles Falconet's *Amour.*

MATUSHKA. No, no. There already was one—the Epirian King, Pyrrhus, the Epirian king, the quintessence of beauty.

BRUCE falls to her knees.

Ancient nicknames have not brought us happiness.

Pause.

Well, that's enough. It's all in the past. Ahead there is only joy.

Pause.

I said immediately—I forgive. Both you and him.

BRUCE. (*Gets up from her knees*). Your mercies, Matushka...

MATUSHKA. To be joyful and happy—that's philosophy.

Pause.

Has His Highness the Prince said anything? About you, me, and the Epirian king—what did he say?

BRUCE. (*rapidly, like a tongue-twister*) That man is not worth her divine love.

MATUSHKA. (*chortles*). Divine! He's incorrigible.

Pause.

Incorrigible. Do you hear?

BRUCE. His Highness says that this youth is excessively and blindly devoted to Matushka.

MATUSHKA. (*Gets absorbed in her manuscript*). Test him.

BRUCE. Test?

MATUSHKA. (*flips through the manuscript*). I don't know what to do with all this. We'll think of something.

Pause.

MATUSHKA hugs BRUCE.

I'm not angry at you. I love you.

BRUCE. (*through tears*). Pyrrhus, the Epirian king.

MATUSHKA. You are the only one with whom I can speak without constraint. The Epirian king, quintessence of beauty. And how many of them were there, those quintessences? How many of them lay behind this mirror.

Pause.

Not so very many. Praise be to the Creator, I am a moral woman, am I not? Not so very many, and all of them unfaithful. All, all unfaithful. Not I to them, but they to me. All to a man.

BRUCE. His Highness the Prince...

MATUSHKA. Don't speak about him now. About his Highness. The learned Grimm wrote me—mein Liebling, it is senseless to keep a desert lion in a cage. So I don't keep them any more. You see yourself how cheerful and calm I am.

BRUCE. So, I am to test this new youth?

MATUSHKA. I shall call him—Sashenka.

Scene Four

Behind the mirror—SASHENKA and BRUCE. SASHENKA lies prone on the bed, face buried in a pillow, BRUCE flits about the room, wiping invisible dust with a feather-duster and keeps looking at SASHENKA. He doesn't move—maybe he is asleep. BRUCE slowly moves over to the desk to the writing-set laid on it...

BRUCE. (*greedily skims it*). Mein Liebe Freunde. I thank you for your attention, your concern. I no longer long for the fine Pyrrhus, the Epirian king, the general whom you know about. I already wrote you, Gnedige Freund, how I discovered this perfidious friend of mine with one of my ladies-in-waiting... the well-known Countess Bruce. Do you remember our favorite sayings of Voltaire from his philosophical tales?

SASHENKA. (*jumping off the bed*). I see you! I see it all!

BRUCE. What a cute sleepy-head you are.

SASHENKA. Put it down! It's not your letter!

BRUCE. (*laughing*). We'll put it down.

SASHENKA. It was Matushka who wrote that. It's not for others to read.

BRUCE. I'm not others.

SASHENKA. You're put here to serve, so serve! Sweep with your duster!

BRUCE. What I'm put here to do, you can't possibly know.

SASHENKA. You're cunning. You're very cunning. I'll tell Matushka.

BRUCE. Tell her.

SASHENKA. Well, I will.

BRUCE. (*laughing*) Tell her.

SASHENKA. Well, I will.

Pause.

(*Sadly*). Matushka won't believe it.

BRUCE. There have been a lot of you behind that mirror.

SASHENKA. A lot?

BRUCE. Think about it.

SASHENKA. I'm not going to think about it. I want to go home.

Pause.

BRUCE. Don't you dare cross me. You better make friends with me. How long you spend lying behind the mirror depends on me.

SASHENKA. It depends on Matushka, on Her will.

BRUCE. You better not cross me... Pyrrhus, the Epirian king, crossed me.

SASHENKA. The Epirian king? That's something out of ancient history.

BRUCE. He was sent to the Smolensk province. He is not to return for a year.

SASHENKA. I wasn't good at ancient history. Papenka gave me the rod for it.

BRUCE. Absence makes the heart forget. That's a proverb. Matushka learns a new proverb every week. Matushka is studying Russian.

SASHENKA. I wasn't good at grammar, either.

BRUCE. He was called the Epirian king because of his beauty. All his proportions were like the ancients, although his ancestry was most plebeian. He didn't even manage to learn how to use a napkin. He was here today, gone tomorrow. He didn't get along with me. Pyrrhus, the Epirian king.

SASHENKA. (*with longing*). I want to go home.

BRUCE. (*moves over to the bed, strokes his head*). Why is it that you don't respect Matushka at all, you don't comfort her?

SASHENKA. I don't know anything. (*Moves away*). I don't know anything. Papa whipped me with the rod for not learning my lessons, and then went and died a sudden death. In our family death always comes early and suddenly. I miss Papa.

BRUCE. Nice, soft hair, silky...

Pause.

Strokes his head.

You find this pleasant, don't you?

Pause.

Don't you cross me. His Highness himself doesn't cross me.

Pause.

This is very pleasant. I know. I've been told.

SASHENKA. (*mechanically*). For grammar he beat me with the rod, for rhetoric he made me stand on my knees on raw peas... for ancient history he yanked me by the hair... I want to go home from here. I really, really want to go home.

BRUCE. Why don't you amuse Matushka, if that's what you're supposed to do?

SASHENKA. (*hurriedly*). My death is also in the near future—an early and rapid death. Once—and it's over. It runs in our family, so that's how it will be for me. I'm no worse than the rest. Since it's been that way for all of them, it will be so for me. I have a mark on my palm.

BRUCE. Matushka scoffs at superstitions and ignorance. Diderot himself writes to her.

SASHENKA. Here it is! There's a cross on my palm, see it? Papa had the same thing. On the very lifeline. And grandpa had it, too.

BRUCE. (*sits next to him on the bed*). Oh, Matushka will explain it all away. If everyone gets vaccinated against smallpox, then enlightenment will ensue and good fortune will be at hand. But this, do you find it pleasant? Everyone finds it pleasant.

SASHENKA. (*perturbed*). My great-grandfather had just got married, just had a son, went off hunting, fell off his horse, broke his neck... Grandpa just married, just had a son, went out sledding, the horses took off, and wolves chewed him up in the night... Papa drunk too much kvas, his stomach swole up...

Pause.

BRUCE. (*ingratiatingly*) And like this? If I touch you like this?

Sashenka jumps up, pushes her away from himself.

SASHENKA. Don't you dare do that! You serve Matushka! Matushka extends her favor to you! And you just twist yourself around, stick your nose into everything, make copies of Matushka's letters! Matushka should have you impaled! She'll give the order—they'll pull out your tongue, draw and quarter you! Don't ever touch me with your hands again!

A creak.

The mirror rises up.

MATUSHKA. Oh, With God's help I have done away with drawing and quartering and no one will have anyone impaled ever again in our Fatherland. We are an enlightened power. I abolished corporal punishment during interrogation. For what is that if not cruelty and ignorance. And indeed Europe is watching us.

BRUCE. (*whispers*). He didn't want to, Matushka... He, alone out of all of them didn't want to...

MATUSHKA. I want to be happy and I am and will be happy. You want to be happy, you are and you will be happy. He wants to be happy, and he will be, and is... Is that how you say it in Russian? I already speak Russian very well.

Scene Five

SASHENKA is alone.

He sprawls on the bed, hair uncombed, barefoot. He gets up, shuffles over to the screen, puts his ear to it,

SASHENKA. (*with disappointment*). Can't hear anything. Can't hear anything.

Throws himself on the bed again, starts to mumble, running his fingers over the page of a book.

...Russia composes a large part of the earth's surface, it is washed by many seas and oceans. Northern and central Russia abounds with rivers and lakes, Southern Russia, with sands and mountains, the easternmost part, with forests and many wild tribes... The innumerable peoples and languages which compose Russia...

Listens again. In irritation sits up and throws the book against the wall.

I can't stand it.

BRUCE appears, quiet and decorous.

BRUCE. Again. That's not nice.

SASHENKA. (*impatiently*). What's going on there? And will it all be over soon?

BRUCE. What do you mean—all?

SASHENKA. All. They locked themselves in and are being secretive.

BRUCE. (*chantingly*). Our Sovereign Matushka is having an audience. Important state information.

SASHENKA. Important state information, and what about me? Just lie here? Till the century ends?

BRUCE. (*wipes off the book and hands it to Sashenka*). That's not nice.

SASHENKA. Till the century ends. I hate geography.

BRUCE. His Highness wrote verses in Latin. Madrigals for Matushka.

SASHENKA. I hate history, too. All the natural sciences.

BRUCE. History is a verbal science. Geography, yes, a natural science. Can't argue with that.

SASHENKA. (*trying to get into the book*). Russia is great with riches, such as: natural ore, shale, and lead, tin, copper and mica, minerals and rich salt mines, where hard-working local residents day and night constantly dig out the very best salt for the needs of all Russia.

Pause.

BRUCE. His Highness is there. He's consoling Matushka. Because the Count died. A famous Count. Once upon a time there was a Count, and then he lost his mind and died.

Pause.

SASHENKA. The very same Count? Matushka's first...

BRUCE. (*waves at him*). Now, now. Who's counting? The First or not. But Matushka did live with him for twelve years.

SASHENKA. (*horrified*) Twelve years? Do things like that really happen?

Pause.

...The very best salt. That I already assimilated. Constantly dig out the very best salt.

Pause.

I won't live for twelve years with anybody. I'm going to die soon.

Pause.

BRUCE. Why must we argue, think about it yourself. You're not a simple one. I respect that most of all in a person. It seems that he's completely open, but no one can understand him.

SASHENKA. I'll die soon, and I don't need anything, take it all away, because I'm going to die soon, because it has been willed so by Fate.

BRUCE. Not a simple one, not simple at all.

Pause.

Nothing is ever simple. You think that I have simply been placed here? You're not simple, you're intelligent, you figured out by whom and why I have been placed here. Why should we quarrel?

Pause.

And how can that be, just—take it all away. How can it be. You've already had quite a bit granted you. A ring for love, and a ruby ring, you've been granted? You've been granted. A hundred thousand gold coins for love. His Highness grinned, "Let him" he said...

SASHENKA. (*nervously*). For what love? For no love. I don't have anything to do with such silliness. At home I had it, in the dove-cote... I crawled up the ladder, and she also crawled up for some reason. And bruised her leg quite a bit.

BRUCE. Who is "she?"

SASHENKA. Somebody. Well, there was this serving-girl. With one squinty-eye. She bruised her leg, so I felt sorry for her. That was at home, in the dove-cote, I had just turned seventeen. She bruised her leg as she climbed the ladder, so I felt sorry for her. And she was very, very dirty, really dirty. But I felt sorry for her. And then repulsed. Why, I said, did you climb the ladder after me, well, why? And she started to cry. And I felt sorry. And she was so, so dirty...

Pause.

And then the time passed, and I left for the service. They say, don't refuse to serve...

Pause.

And that was all! And nothing more! And all my loving. I really don't like to do all this.

Pause.

BRUCE. (*insinuatingly*). And what about Matushka?
SASHENKA. And I said—let me go. The ring! The ring, they say. The gold coins! What is it to me, if my fate is already decided?
BRUCE. And how does Matushka take it, if you behave that way?
SASHENKA. What about Matushka, she's forever sitting on the throne. Matushka's husband died an evil death, and it's nothing to her, she rules. Matushka's Count died recently, and it's still nothing. Matushka knows and understands absolutely everything better than anybody else. And she's superhumanly educated. And I, I don't like to do stupid things. And my fate is already decided.
BRUCE. It's actually his Highness who set you up with Matushka, His Highness.
SASHENKA. It's not nice to do stupid things in general. I remember, in the dove-cote. And Matushka shines in glory. How can I encroach on greatness?

The mirror rises.
MATUSHKA, disheveled, is weeping.

MATUSHKA. (*prostrate*) Mein gnedige Freund. The count has died, but my eyes are dry. I loved him so. My friend, where is it all now, where is this love, where, where?

Pause.

She calls:

Katerina Ivanovna! Where are you, Katerina Ivanovna?

Sobs.

How badly you work, Katerina Ivanovna. You're my chamber-maid, you serve me, and you're never where you're supposed to be. Never, if I need you. It's going to be a disaster when you get married, Katerina Ivanovna! Your husband will beat you.

Pause.

My husband also beat me. And the Count beat me. The deceased Count. Why am I not crying?

Pause.

Why hasn't anyone ever loved me, why?

Pause.

 My husband beat me, and spit on me, and pinched me in bed, and there were huge dogs howling around us. He would throw them pieces of meat and laugh. And I would lie in bed alone and every night, every night I would hope that everything would be different...

Pause.

 Katerina Ivanovna! Where are you! Better never, never, try to please your husband, Katerina Ivanovna...

Pause.

BRUCE. (*in a whisper*). His Highness the Prince...
MATUSHKA. You mustn't! Be silent!

Pause.

 No one loved me, not ever, and no one ever will. I loved, I was capable of it. You, he said, are impossible to love, you're a freak, not a woman...
SASHENKA. (*takes her by the hand, softly*). Aurora...
MATUSHKA. You mustn't! Don't call me that! They all... all...

Pause.

Matushka weeps, Bruce, carefully undresses her.

SASHENKA. I begged to go home... Well, so what... I can go home later... I'll stay here, if you need me... I feel very good here... I feel very, very good...

Pause.

 I like it here, behind the mirror... I don't feel like going anywhere else. I know anyhow how it will all end. But in the meantime, so what, it's behind the mirror for me. If you feel calmer that way. Knowing that I'm always here, behind the mirror.

Pause.

Sashenka takes her by the hand. Matushka fitfully embraces him.

MATUSHKA. (*dully*) God save you, if I fall in love with you. May God save you if that happens.

PART II

The mirror is up.

Matushka in a night-cap sits at her desk, writing. Sashenka is lying on the bed.

He's bored. Pulls on the tassels on the pillows, studies his hands, yawns, covering his mouth.

SASHENKA. (*mutters, forgetfully*) (nursery rhyme) A bag rolled down a great hunch-back hill. In the bag is bread-salt-water-grain. Who wants to share it?

MATUSHKA. What? What are you saying?

SASHENKA. Nothing. Just talking to myself.

MATUSHKA. (*reading what she has written*) ...Two days ago, on Thursday, February 9th was the fortieth anniversary of when I first arrived in Moscow with my mother. I think that here in St. Petersburg you couldn't find even ten people alive who remember my arrival... (*tearing herself away, caressingly*) What are you saying.

SASHENKA. Me? Nothing.

MATUSHKA. Down what back?

SASHENKA. Down a great hunch-back.

MATUSHKA. Down a great hunch-back? What's that?

SASHENKA. It's a saying. That's just how it goes.

Pause.

MATUSHKA. But what kind of a bag is it?

Pause.

You ought to do something, Sashenka.

Pause.

SASHENKA. (*indefinitely*). I do things. I read. I've read so much already.

Pause.

MATUSHKA. Can you really be bored, Sashenka?

Pause.

...Who remember my arrival... But you're not bored, are you?

Long pause.

Sashenka!

SASHENKA. I'm fine.

MATUSHKA. Yes, yes. An enlightened person can never be bored. For example, the learned Grimm, mein lieber Freund, writes me, and asks, how is it that I am never, ever bored. I answer why: because I passionately love to be busy and find that a person is only happy when he is busy. Isn't that true?

SASHENKA. (*quietly*) Bread-salt-water-grain... Russia is abundant in great riches... It is a large expanse of land...

MATUSHKA. So you're studying geography, that's a smart fellow.

Pause.

The Empress Elizabeth... do you know... she didn't know geography at all. She didn't believe that England was an island. Didn't believe it, refused to believe, and then she died.

SASHENKA. (*stunned*). England? An island? What a misery. To live on an island.

Pause. Decisively.

And yesterday I—went for a walk in the Winter Garden.

MATUSHKA. (*scowling*). In the Winter Garden. That's good.

Pause.

Going for walks—is healthy.

Pause.

SASHENKA. But I only went into the Winter Garden!

Pause.

I don't have to go walk in the Winter Garden anymore. I don't care.

Pause.

MATUSHKA. I'm so glad that you're not bored here. So glad.

Pause.

The Empress Elizabeth also kept asking me, "aren't you bored here, little girl?" And she'd give me a ginger-bread cookie. Or a puppy. "You," she would say, little girl, never go for walks, you, she would say, are going to read your eyes out."

Pause.

Three days ago I wrote Diderot about it.

SASHENKA. (*quietly*). I bag rolled down a great hunch-back... A bag rolled down a great hunch-back... In this bag was bread—salt--water--grain... Who wants to share it...

MATUSHKA. Oh, I valued philosophy greatly, because my soul was always truly Republican.

SASHENKA. (*whispers*) Who do you want to share it with? Say right away, don't deceive the good, kind people.

MATUSHKA. (*looks at her notes, with enthusiasm*) Never has the universe produced a braver, more positive, open, humane, kind, benevolent, generous person than the Russian. Not one man of another race can compare with him in the beauty and regularity of his features, in the freshness of his skin, in the breadth of his shoulders, his build, and height. His simpleheartedness and honesty defend him from vices. He is quick and exact in his obedience and loyal.

Pause.

(*In an altered voice*). Sashenka.

SASHENKA. (*after a pause*). What is it Matushka, whatever you wish.

MATUSHKA. Sashenka... How glorious! How glorious it is for us here!

SASHENKA. Yes, Matushka.

MATUSHKA. It's glorious for us, for you and me, alone here together.

Pause.

Your little head doesn't ache any more, does it? Your little head doesn't ache as much.

Pause.

You are completely, completely different. Be silent. Oh, yes, it has seemed that way to me every time. My heart has not learned to live without love, and every time it has seemed different to me. But you are completely, completely different.

Pause.

You won't go again, without my permission, into the Winter Garden, will you?

Pause.

You never know what can happen in the Winter Garden. It's drafty, and you had a sore throat. There are tropical plants, and they exude fumes at night. There are tomatoes-- poisonous Italian fruits-- and you might suddenly feel like trying them. There are my Freulein, my chamber-maids, like that Katerina Ivanovna, my Kalmyk girl, she might drop by, and she's young and stupid. You never know what might happen in the Winter Garden. It's very dangerous to walk there.

SASHENKA. (*meekly*). I won't go anywhere. If it's unpleasant for you. Anyway, I am fated to die soon.

MATUSHKA. Being superstitious is laughable in our century, simply ridiculous. You're silly, Sasha, you're simply silly. You didn't even finish reading Montesquieu's "Spirit of the Laws". And Helvetius you didn't finish reading. You didn't even open it, I know, that Helvetius! Otherwise you would know, that those are ridiculous, absurd superstitions and no evil fate exists.

The tap of heels is heard. Countess Bruce flits in.

BRUCE. (*curtseys*) Matushka… excuse me…

MATUSHKA. Oh, I told you. Never disturb me during my rest hours. Never.

BRUCE. Matushka, but His Highness the Prince is waiting. He begs to enter.

MATUSHKA. Then let him enter, if there's no help for it.

Pause.

But better tomorrow. I also have to rest sometimes. I'm a human being just like the rest. I'm resting.

BRUCE. (*seems to remind her*) His Highness!

MATUSHKA. Well, all right, let him come in.

Pause.

Well, what's the matter?

BRUCE. (*significantly*). He… His Highness… wants to be alone… As it used to be, to behold Matushka alone.

MATUSHKA. What does it matter how it used to be?

BRUCE. It is his Highness's request, to meet alone.

Pause.

MATUSHKA. But I'm resting! He rests sometimes? Doesn't he? And nobody disturbs him. The desert lion feels confined in a cage, so fine. But some don't find it confining. I, my friend, don't bother him, so let it be as he sees best. Everything as he sees best, and I never bother him, never. If that's the way he needs it to be.

BRUCE. (*quietly*)That's the way they all need it to be.

MATUSHKA. Not all! Not all! There are those who aren't unfaithful.

BRUCE. And who is so glorious as that?

MATUSHKA. There are those who aren't unfaithful, who don't deceive. There are those who are always the same, true and constant.

BRUCE. But he was seen walking in the Winter Garden. Sniffing the flowers.

MATUSHKA. And what of it—the Winter Garden. I know better than you do about the Winter Garden. And he won't go there any more.

BRUCE. And that's how it will be - always behind the mirror, and that's all? And won't go anywhere?

MATUSHKA. If someone is happy, when one thinks of him, then why go far away?

Pause.

BRUCE. He's crying, His Highness the Prince. He says its unbearable. He has state matters to discuss. Of importance to the State.

MATUSHKA. (*excitedly*). It's too late! Everything has already been decided!

BRUCE. He says—she, he says, has always been generous to me.

Pause. Matushka, after thinking it over, makes a sign with her hand, and the mirror falls, hiding her, leaving Sashenka and Bruce in a tete-a-tete.

SASHENKA. What is this?

BRUCE. (*shrugging her shoulders*). His Highness.

Pause.

His word is law. What ever he says, Matushka will give in to him. That's the way it's been, that's the way it is and will be, amen.

SASHENKA. (*jumps up, knocks with his fists against the screen*). No!

Pause.

BRUCE. (*laughs*). Yes.

SASHENKA. (*bewildered*) She... Matushka... she said, today we won't receive anyone, just you, we'll be together... You and I... She said so...

BRUCE. (*insistently*). You just think about it. She said so, and you just think about it. You will still have to live on and on.
It's your fourth year here? Is this good?

SASHENKA. Matushka says that she doesn't need any one else.

Pause.

She doesn't need anyone else, only me, such as I am. And what am I.

Pause.

She says... what of it, Matushka knows how to appreciate men, everyone knows that. So, I'm just fine.

BRUCE. So she says, but you think about it. Think about it.

Pause.

Who put you here behind the mirror?

SASHENKA. (*pressing his ear to the screen*) They're saying... What is it they're saying?

BRUCE. His Highness knew that Matushka likes a bogatyr's build and amazing boldness. That's what you were put here for, so that you wouldn't stay long. IIis Highness doesn't like it when somebody stays here for a long time. That's why he picked you. And see what has happened.

SASHENKA. (*challengingly*). Matushka said—she's going to marry me.

BRUCE. (*not smiling*). You're lying.

SASHENKA. For sixteen years, she said, I suffered with a Holstein freak, the chance came along to resolve it... She didn't marry the Count, she didn't marry His Highness, but she'll marry me.

BRUCE. (*simply*). Tell me you're lying.

Pause.

SASHENKA. And as for me, well, let her marry me, if she feels like it. I already know my fate, anyway. Let her marry me, it's even more fun that way.

BRUCE. His Highness doesn't know anything about this.

SASHENKA. And now he'll find out? He'll find out, won't he! So that's the way it is!

BRUCE. Tell me you've been lying.

Pause.

I feel sorry for you. I've grown accustomed to you.

SASHENKA. Well, then, don't tell him! What do you think!

BRUCE. I feel sorry for you.

SASHENKA. (*listening, his ear to the screen*) They were talking, now they've stopped. What are they doing there?

Pause.

What, what are they doing there?

BRUCE. Sashenka... You listen to me now.

SASHENKA. Can it really all be true, what they say about her?

BRUCE. There was a deputation that passed... through that hall... Where Matushka's bed is... and the Swedish ambassador said, Your Majesty, what kind of room is behind that mirror. What is it hiding? And they were talking about your room, Sashenka, about this one.

SASHENKA. (*finally moves away from the screen, sullenly*). Well?

BRUCE. And Matushka up and says: there, she says, as you can see, is a chamber-pot.

SASHENKA. (*destroyed*). A chamber-pot.

BRUCE. A chamber-pot, and I take it out whenever I want, from behind the mirror. For my big needs and my little ones...

Sashenka is silent.

And everyone laughed so hard, they laughed so hard...

Pause.

His Highness - he's a wise one. He's kind, his Highness. He's kind to everyone, even to you. Give him, that Sashenka—that's what he says to me, give him, my dear—that's what he says to me some times, my dear, he says to me, give him...

Pause.

Here's—some clothing. A Preobrazhensky officer's uniform. Here's some money. Katerina Ivanovna will lead you out of here by that staircase. Below there's a lackey with a horse, he knows where to go. And—just vanish into thin air.

Pause.

Evil fate is like a woman, you can always run away from her, that's what His Highness bid me tell you.

She leaves.

Sashenka is alone. He lies down on the bed, takes a book, flips through it. Jumps up, whirls around the room, doesn't know what to do with himself. Puts his ear to the screen. Pulls on the Preobrzhensky officer's uniform, the three-cornered hat... Takes the purse with money. And with rapid steps exits the room.

Scene Six

The mirror is raised.

Matushka is alone, at her desk.

MATUSHKA. Mein liebe freund. My learned and highly esteemed friend. Your discussion of the encyclopedists and moralists is brilliant. I wrote my commentary on it in letter number twenty-nine and sent a copy to Monsieur Diderot...

(*Puts her head down on the top of the desk, weeps.*)

BRUCE. (*entering*) Again, Matushka, is this seemly?

MATUSHKA. I'm merry. I'm calm and merry.

Pause.

You know me.

BRUCE. (*indefinitely*) Oh, I know you, Matushka.

MATUSHKA. All I need is to decide something. I told you... you could read in my Notes...

BRUCE. Oh, your Notes!

MATUSHKA. Yes, I'm willing them to you... to my only friend...

Bruce kisses her hand.

You remember how when I was almost still a stupid girl, how I reasoned about my husband. He was not yet Peter III then, but the Royal Prince. And I was the Royal Princess. "Just think," I said to myself, "you are always going to be unhappy here. Your husband is ready to love any woman except you. Even the hunchbacked Princess Kurlyandskaya, even the pock-marked Liza Vorontsova. Your husband is going to commit infidelities to spite you. To love such a husband is to be eternally jealous, be eternally unhappy. And I decided to stop loving my husband, in order not to make myself unhappy.

Pause.

I want to become happy. I want the whole, whole country to become happy. I want that all to come to be. When manners become more refined and laws triumph. And until then I must work, work...

BRUCE. (*with pity*) Matushka. He's not worth it.

MATUSHKA. A young man leaves for his native estate, to take up agriculture, that's a most common occurrence. I myself signed the decree "On the Liberty of the Gentry". It's possible to serve, and its also possible to become a useful member of society in the remote countryside.

BRUCE. (*in a whisper*). There was nothing interesting about him, no substance at all. He was just pitiful.

Pause.

But what about that fine young fellow who brought the firewood this morning... did you see him?

Pause. Matushka is silent.

That means, you saw him.

Pause.

What a looker, eh? What blazing red cheeks! And what shoulders! Just your taste. He carried the firewood. Now every morning he'll bring you firewood for the fireplace.

Pause.

Well, why are you silent, Matushka? Isn't he good-looking enough?

MATUSHKA. Did His Highness appoint him to me?

BRUCE. Just your taste, bursting with strength, absolutely blooming with health. That's your taste, isn't it, Matushka, as it used to be?

Pause.

MATUSHKA. (*bursting into tears*) Sashenka, Sashenka...

BRUCE. What of Sashenka now?

They are silent.

MATUSHKA. Only one thing I can't seem to figure out—what am I to do with the Ukrainian deputation. His Highness has contradicted me again, and everyone has gotten mixed up in the question.

Pause.

BRUCE. (*sadly*). But I heard, that their marshall's sister isn't nearly as pretty as they say.

MATUSHKA. But they do say that she is pretty.

BRUCE. Not so very. Not so very pretty. He'll soon get sick of her. If everyone says, that she's not pretty.

MATUSHKA. Not UNpretty, just not so very pretty.

BRUCE. Everyone says so. I heard it.

MATUSHKA. On the other hand, she is young.

BRUCE. He'll get sick of her soon, if she's not so very pretty, if everyone says so.

Pause.

He'll get sick of her soon, that's what always happens.

MATUSHKA. (*reading aloud*). You will try from the very first moment that these provinces come beneath our scepter to put an end to all the persecutions, repressions, injustices, brigandry, murders, and cruel tortures during judicial investigation, and also to executions and horrible punishments. There is one means, one true means to soften the mores of these people: trade and the comforts of life...

BRUCE. That's the way it always happens. One thing after another.

Noise. Knocking. Someone is knocking on the walls of the hall.

After a minute, Sashenka appears.

SASHENKA. Here I am. Here I am in person.

Matushka screams.

Don't refuse to serve. Don't ask to serve. Don't refuse to serve, don't ask to serve, the service will find you itself.

Matushka in tears throws her arms around his neck.

All of us in our family have suffered a sudden and unjust death. So let it be so.

MATUSHKA. (*whispers distractedly*) Oh, mein Leibling... Oh...

BRUCE. (*fussing about*) I... for just a minute... I'll go look for Katerina Ivanovna... Katerina Ivanovna doesn't serve you at all, she's so negligent... The Kalmyks are a very diligent nation, but she - is quite negligent... And she's to be married...

MATUSHKA. Sashenka, if you die, then I shall die too. Know that. If you go, then I will go after you...

BRUCE. (*excitedly*) She's to be married, Katerina Ivanovna, for Matushka is giving her in marriage... to a fine man... (*sidles sideways, creeps to the exit*)

MATUSHKA Listen to me, Praskovia. Stop, and listen to me. I have great joy. He is - my fiance, Sashenka. My fiance, General Lanskoi. You're a general now, Sashenka. Haven't I told you?

Scene Seven

Behind the mirror.

Matushka and Sashenka, together. Then in the darkness

Countess Bruce steals in.

MATUSHKA. (*lively*). I hate lotteries. I prohibited lotteries in my state, it's completely dishonest dealing with fate. Now the age of science has begun, the age of philosophy, the age of liberty. There's something pitiful, savage, low about lotteries. I really, really loved the Russian proverb. How does it go? Believe in God, but don't slip up yourself. How expressive Russian proverbs are. How remarkable the Russian language is!

Pause.

You know, our love would be completely different, if we spoke a different language. It's good that you don't know German. When you speak Russian, love changes, too. We're lucky.

Sashenka slides off the bed, runs into Countess Bruce.

SASHENKA. It's you?
BRUCE. Here, I've brought something to drink.
SASHENKA. To drink? For Matushka?
BRUCE. No, no. Not for Matushka. For you. Katerina Ivanovna prepared it.
SASHENKA. And where is Katerina Ivanovna?
BRUCE. She's coming soon. She prepared a drink for you. Their national beverage. For potency.

Pause. Sashenka takes the cup.

SASHENKA. And that's all?
BRUCE. From it a man's potential for love becomes inexhaustible.
SASHENKA. (*taking the cup*) You know I really don't like engaging in such silliness.
MATUSHKA. My friends, I intend to read you my epitaph. I wrote it to make fun of superstitions. I firmly intend to live twenty-five more years, to behold the dawn of a totally new century. Thus—here lies the body of Katherine the Second, born in Shtettin on the 21st of April, 1729. She came to Russia to marry Peter the Third. For fourteen years she composed a plan, a triple plan: to please her husband, Empress Elizabeth, and the people—and she forgot nothing in order to attain success in this. Eighteen years of boredom and loneliness forced her to read a great deal... Are you listening to me?
BRUCE. (*to Sashenka*) But his Highness could make love to a woman all night.
SASHENKA. And with Matushka? How was it for him with Matushka?
BRUCE. (*mumbles*) It was, is and shall be, amen.
MATUSHKA. Further. Ascending to the Russian throne, she desired the best and tried to grant her subjects happiness, liberty, and property; she willingly forgave and hated no one...
SASHENKA. (*takes the cup*) All night, then? So I should drink this, should I? You tell me, it's a good drink, it helps?

MATUSHKA. Indulgent, full of joie de vivre, cheerful by nature, with the soul of a republican and a kind heart, she had many friends. Work was easy for her. She liked society and art.

SASHENKA. It helps?

Drinks it in one gulp. Then crawls again into bed beside Matushka. Bruce sits in the corner, waits to see what will happen...

MATUSHKA. Are you asleep? No? I also don't feel like sleeping for some reason. Too much joy. An excess of feeling always excites one. So listen, I was in the theater yesterday, I already started to tell you about it, my Sashenka, my love, mein Leibling. You know, All this doesn't encourage talents, but perverts them. I myself tried writing plays, I know about it. In Paris itself they perform no better than here. Because the public abandons good theater for bad; in comedies, they mix laughter with tears; and as for tragedies, they perform only horror stories. And those who can't write comedies that cause laughter, or tragedies that make one weep—write only dramas... I was, as I already told you, in the theater last night. They performed tolerably well, but it was of so little use... Did you fall asleep? Are you sleeping? That's fine, sleep. I'll tell you the plot of the play when you wake up.

In the meantime it has gotten darker and darker. Finally Bruce blows out the candle, and it becomes completely dark...

Scene Eight

The same hall, as in the beginning of the act. Countess Bruce is alone. She removes the funeral decorations, returns the setting to its festive appearance. And again she rushes, sideways, sidling—to the open desk, to the unfinished letter, to the as yet unknown secrets.

BRUCE (*grabs the letter, reads greedily*) Mein Gnedige Freund. For five months I have day and night been in the thrall of obsessive memories, I weep over my loss. A week after my last letter to you, Fedor Orlov and Prince Potemkin came to me. Before that moment I could not bear the sight of a human face; but they had it well figured—they began to wail with me, and then it became easier for me to bear. By force of my sensitivity I became a creature without any feeling for anything, excepting this grief; it became stronger, was sustained by memories with every step I took in my room and with every word. Finally, there began to be a few intervals: first a few calm hours, then—days... only don't think, mein liebe Freund, that the loss of General Lanskoi forced me to forget my duty. In my horrible condition I did not neglect the smallest business which demanded my attention. During those terrible minutes, orders were expected from me, and I gave them correctly and reasonably, which especially struck General Saltykov...

Gradually the hall takes on its former festive appearance. The mourning period has ended. Music plays, drowning out the last words of the letter.

Countess Bruce, bidding farewell, makes a deep curtsey.

Olga Mikhailova

Olga Mikhailova

RUSSIAN DREAM

A Comedy Without an Intermission

DRAMATIS PERSONNAE

KIMBERLEY
ILYA
ANASTASIA PETROVNA, Ilya's grandmother
NIUSHA, a neighbor of Ilya's
VOVA, another neighbor of Ilya's
MARTHA

RUSSIAN DREAM

Once upon a time in a far-off land in a kingdom whose capital city was called Moscow, there stood a house, neither small nor large, whose paint was faded and whose plaster was crumbling, but whose circular staircase held firm and around it wound a wrought-iron bannister in the style of art moderne. On the top floor, since the before the war, lived Anastasia Petrovna. With her lived her grandson Ilya, her neighbor Niusha and her other neighbor Vova. And that was all, so living was manageable. True, the apartment had become a bit ramshackle during the untended communal years, as had the entire house. Repairs had long been promised by the authorities, for which the exterior of the house was surrounded by scaffolding (on which here and there had already sprouted slender Russian birches), and inside the apartment had been placed carpenter's horses. On the horses, as on the stair-landings all kinds of junk had piled up, which evoked a nagging feeling in the heart and therefore had not been taken off to the flea-market.

Anastasia Petrovna was retired now, and considered herself to have every right not to work. But in bygone years she had given the children English lessons. Therefore Iliusha and the neighbor-girl Niusha (tutored in childhood free of charge so that her parents wouldn't report on the illegal lessons to the authorities) could speak a bit of English. This ability, however obligatory within the borders of the United States, in Russia was absolutely inessential and even unpleasant.

Neighbor Vova—a man of indeterminate age—knew no English and had no desire to learn. Although his room was the farthest down the hall, it nevertheless fell to his lot to open the door (thirty five steps to the door and thirty-five back again.) Anastasia Petrovna had no interest in the ringing of doorbells, Niusha always played loud music and therefore heard no outside sounds, and Ilya was too lazy. Ilya's room was the closest to the entrance. To avoid opening the door to his room as well, he set Vova the task of boring a hole through which he extended a rope which was attached to the door-hook. Not an elaborate device, but how it made life easier! Pull the rope, and the door would open.

Ilya's room is large, but seems crowded due to the innumerable objects contained in it. To avoid going anywhere, he collected everything that might possibly prove necessary: a wardrobe cabinet, a bookshelf, a cabinet to store china and foodstuffs, a refrigerator for those foodstuffs that might go bad in the cabinet, a writing-table to make study possible and a dining-table, to have a meal once in a while, and finally, a large ottoman not only for sleeping but for general living. The only missing item was a stove, but Ilya was not trained to do any cooking himself, and ate hot food only when it was brought him by his grandmother or Niusha. And he had a heating-coil for tea. Since walking down the long corridor for water was a burdensome process, Ilya kept a supply in a large pitcher. When the pitcher was empty, silver spoons inside it would clink: grandmother had thrown them in—water becomes cleaner and tastier from contact with silver. The water in Moscow used to be extraordinarily tasty, but it's gotten worse,—Anastasia Petrovna would say.

It is now late in the evening. Ilya lies on his ottoman, covered so that only the top of his head sticks out. His grandmother sits beside him.

ANASTASIA PETROVNA. In the olden days, when God's earth was inhabited with wood-demons, water-sprites, and mermaids, when the rivers ran with milk and honey and the fields were filled with flying roast fowl, there lived Queen Anastasia the Fair with her Grandson Prince Ilya.

ILYA. He was a bachelor without a wife.

ANASTASIA PETROVNA. And he wished to marry only the foreign princess Militrisa Kirbitevna.

ILYA. And was she the fairest of the fair?

ANASTASIA PETROVNA. Beyond a doubt. On her forehead shone a star, beneath her braid gleamed the moon.

ILYA. (*sitting up*) I should leap on my finest steed and ride in search of her.

ANASTASIA PETROVNA. (*tucking him in for the night*). What is your rush? Lie down, better go to sleep, things will turn out for the best. Morning is wiser than evening.

Thank God, they lived through the night till morning. Ilya and Kimberley are lying on the ottoman under a thick down comforter. And outside the tall windows in the streets it is the very beginning of the 1980s.

ILYA. "And oft when on my couch I lie..."

KIMBERLEY. (*waking up*). What's it now?

ILYA. December with a long white beard.

KIMBERLEY. No, what time of day is it? I've gotten everything all mixed up.

ILYA. It's morning.

KIMBERLEY. Then why is it dark out?

ILYA. They've already turned off the streetlights, and it's still dark, so that means it's after 9 a.m.

KIMBERLEY. They're probably looking for me.

ILYA. Who's looking?

KIMBERLEY. Martha.

ILYA. Who's Martha?

KIMBERLEY. The lady from the embassy, daddy's friend, whom I'm supposed to be visiting.

ILYA. Ah... well, let her look.

KIMBERLEY. She probably thinks I've been nabbed by the KGB.

ILYA. What does the KGB need you for?

KIMBERLEY. What do you mean? A foreigner, first time in Moscow, heads straight for a certain address and dissappears for the entire night. What else can they think? A spy!

ILYA. Ah, well, let her think that.

KIMBERLEY. And if she finds me?

ILYA. It's dark out. She won't find you.

KIMBERLEY. But what if she does?

ILYA. Well, let her.

KIMBERLEY. Then we better get up. Is it always so cold when you get up in the morning? Coming out from under the covers is awful.

ILYA. No, not always. Only in fall, winter, and spring.

KIMBERLEY. Don't you feel the cold? Yesterday I saw a very young girl eating ice cream in the street!

ILYA. We most definitely feel it. But ice-cream, well, if they've already invented ice-cream, then somebody has to eat it.

KIMBERLEY. And how do you manage in the morning?

ILYA. We don't. We just don't get up. In any case, in winter that's the simplest way.

KIMBERLEY. I'm so happy that I got away for the Christmas vacation and came here. Christmas in America is so trivial, you just can't imagine.

ILYA. Of course I can't imagine. They did away with Christmas here before I was born.

KIMBERLEY. It's so neat here. Snow all over the streets, real snow-drifts.

ILYA. There's always snow in winter, Kimberley, that's the way it's supposed to be. The cycle of nature, water turns to snow. Or didn't they teach you that in school?

KIMBERLEY. What do you mean, they didn't teach us? They taught us about it. Only I've never seen snow in the city before.

ILYA. It's my present to you.

KIMBERLEY. Thank you. It's a good thing I brought my warmest clothes with me. Now Martha's going to hunt me down, drag me off to the theater. There's an American theater troupe on tour here, did you know? Everybody's going to be there tonight. Martha yelled at me for not bringing any dress-up clothes. She's going to stick her dresses on me! Ugh! Shall we go?

ILYA. No. I know what your theater's like, noise, yelling, running around. Art should be thoughtful.

KIMBERLEY. I'm hungry.

ILYA. There's a roast bull standing on the seashore, he's got a sharp knife in his side, cut a slice and eat it.

KIMBERLEY. On what shore?

ILYA. Let's have a drink first to warm up, then it will be warm enough for breakfast.

KIMBERLEY. A drink of what?

ILYA. Of vodka. I have here... (*he gets a little flask out from somewhere*).

KIMBERLEY. We'll have to get up to get some glasses anyway.

ILYA. You see, the top isn't metal, it's plastic, so that you can drink when it's freezing out. Vova gave it to me.

KIMBERLEY. Who's Vova?

ILYA. My neighbor. He lives in our apartment, closer to the kitchen. It's warm in his room, because of the oven.

KIMBERLEY. Is he a relative?

ILYA. No, just a neighbor. But he knows how to do just about eveything.

KIMBERLEY. But why does he live in your apartment?

ILYA. It's a communal apartment.

KIMBERLEY. How interesting! And are there other unrelated people here?

ILYA. Yes, there's a girl, Niusha.

KIMBERLEY. How neat! I hate bourgeois middle-class living. But you have an amazing apartment, it's just like a cave in a fairy-tale.

ILYA. Aw, it's not much, it's an OK life.

Knock on the door.

KIMBERLEY. Who's that knocking?

ILYA. I don't know. It could be just about anybody, they all get up early around here.

Repeated knock.

KIMBERLEY. Don't open it. Let's just be alone, just the two of us. We haven't kissed even once in the morning, you know. We've had evening kisses, night-time kisses, but no morning ones...

VOVA. (*behind the door*). You may be quiet as a mouse, Iliusha, but I still hear you, so I'm pulling on the rope.

Vova pulls the rope, the door opens, and Vova drags into the room a large eccentric cage, almost as tall as a person, thus taking up all the remaining space in the room.

VOVA. There! My crowning achievement. What do you think? (*notices Kimberley*). Ah, so you're not alone. Well, that's OK, let the young damsel have a look, too.

KIMBERLEY. What's he saying?

ILYA. He's greeting us.

KIMBERLEY. Hello!

VOVA. Oh, you've dragged a non-Russian into bed with you and you're drinking wine with her. Treat your neighbor to celebrate the end of his labors—I've spent three months on this fucking thing.

KIMBERLEY. What's he saying?

ILYA. That he spent three months making this cage.

VOVA. (*takes the cap of the vodka bottle from Ilya, sits down on the edge of the ottoman*). Oh, let the nectar of the Gods flow all round! Fill my cup, I'll drink to anybody, even a Tatar princess!

ILYA. She's American.

VOVA. What the devil!

ILYA. He's drinking to your health, Kimberley.

KIMBERLEY. Thank you.

VOVA. From the States, eh? We understand. Once upon a time lived a fox and a bunny-rabbit. The fox had a hut of ice, and the rabbit of wood. So the fox jumped lickety-split under the covers with the rabbit!

KIMBERLEY. What do you need such a big cage for?

ILYA. Yes, Vova, what do you need such a big cage for?

VOVA. Isn't it grand? I worked for three months, spent fifteen hundred on materials alone. Sold my overcoat.

ILYA. And what are you doing to do with it now?

VOVA. I don't know.

ILYA. But how did you ever think up something that size?

VOVA. At the clinic we have a giant aloe plant that looks something like a chicken, if you look at it from the back, only larger, like an ostrich, but with no legs, you get it?

ILYA. Kimberley, this cage is made for a palm tree.

KIMBERLEY. Do you usually keep palm trees in cages here?

ILYA. We don't have palm trees.

KIMBERLEY. Did he make it for foreign export?

Knock at the door.

ILYA. Pull the rope, pull it.

Niusha enters.

NIUSHA. "I wandered lonely as a cloud..." I was walking along and heard my beloved English language. Who is it you're talking so fluently with, Ilya?

ILYA. With Vova.

NIUSHA. No, who have you got in bed with you?

ILYA. A doll.

NIUSHA. You didn't sleep with dolls even when you were a kid. You had a teddy-bear, I remember, but no dollie.

KIMBERLEY: (*sticks her head out from under the covers*). I'm Kimberley.

NIUSHA. A real looker. A genuine American beauty rose.

KIMBERLEY. You think I look like an American?

NIUSHA. Yes, indeed. And you speak fantastic English, as if it were your native language.

VOVA. Why don't you react to my cage?

NIUSHA. I was just about to say that the last exit has become blocked.

VOVA. All you women are twits, you look at things from a funny angle. This is a major feat of engineering, it has the same safety factor as a railroad bridge. Go ahead, crawl in, it'll hold. I guarantee you.

NIUSHA. Crawl in? What for?

ILYA. And what did you come here for? To shoot the breeze. Drink vodka.

NIUSHA. No, I had a reason for coming... I don't remember.

Knock at the door.

ANASTASIA PETROVNA. Ilusha, I hear you, have they waked you up already?

ILYA. Good morning, grandmother. Yes, I'm awake.

ANASTASIA PETROVNA. I've made you breakfast.

ILYA. And what have you made?

ANASTASIA PETROVNA. Oatmeal.

ILYA. I won't eat oatmeal! Let the dogs eat oatmeal!

VOVA. The wee hours of the morning and they're speaking English! Lord, why have you heaped such neighbors upon me?

ANASTASIA PETROVNA. Oatmeal is very good for your health, that's why our brand is called "Hercules."

ILYA. I don't want to be a Hercules.

ANASTASIA PETROVNA. But you can eat just a little for grandma's sake. I'll bring you some.

ILYA. I'm not alone.

ANASTASIA PETROVNA. And how many of you are there?

ILYA. Two. Not including Vova and Niusha.

ANASTASIA PETROVNA. In that case I'll bring two bowls.

A ring of the doorbell. Anastasia Petrovna, completely unflustered, goes out to the kitchen. No one moves in the room. Pause. The doorbell rings again.

VOVA. Niusha, go open the door, you're standing closest to it.

NIUSHA. Why don't you crawl through your cage and check its weight resistance?

VOVA. What's to check? It's made to last centuries.

The doorbell rings again.

VOVA. What kind of people are you anyway? Somebody's gotta open the door.

NIUSHA. Whoever feels the need to open it, let him open it.

The doorbell rings again.

ILYA. You think I should get up myself and open the door?

KIMBERLEY. Why doesn't anyone open the door? Has somebody come you don't want to see?

ILYA. How should we know who's come? Nobody's up to answering the door.

The doorbell rings again.

VOVA. Well, I'm coming, I'm coming. (*he crawls through the cage, goes out, opens the entrance-door and lets in Martha.*)

MARTHA. I'd like to know... I don't know if I've come to the right place?....

VOVA. Heavens, and what a fine odor you have. Like a bouquet of fragrant prairie-blossoms.

MARTHA. You like it?

VOVA. If you turn down the power on it, it's OK.

ANASTASIA PETROVNA. (*walking through the corridor towards Ilya's room*). Vova, don't keep the lady standing on the threshhold.

VOVA. Who's keeping her? I haven't even laid a finger on her. Besides, she's of indeterminate nationality.

MARTHA. What did the lady say, I didn't catch it?

VOVA. Of course, you didn't. You break into a stranger's home... There's only one word for that. *Inorodka.*

ANASTASIA PETROVNA. (*Already in the room*). Here's your cereal. For you and your girlfriend.

ILYA. Let me introduce you, grandma, this is Kimberley. She came here straight from the USA.

ANASTASIA PETROVNA. Straight from the USA? Into your bed? Well, let her eat oatmeal.

KIMBERLEY. I didn't come straight into bed, I came straight to the apartment.

ILYA. She came to our apartment, grandma. To take a look.

ANASTASIA PETROVNA. And our apartment is famous in America? It's mentioned in their guidebooks?

KIMBERLEY. It's the apartment of my great-grandfather.

NIUSHA. So you're a real-live American? And you've come to claim our apartment?

MARTHA (*in the corridor*). I don't know the word "Inorodka". I know "urodka." And it means "freak."

VOVA. You're no freak, you're fine as a woman in the generic sense, but your nationality...

MARTHA. I'm American by nationality. What's so bad about that?

VOVA. It's a nationality like any other. Although it's got a rather bad reputation in Russia. But in a nationality itself there's nothing good or bad. It's like a fish in the sea—as long as it's swimming, it has no flavor. But once you make personal contact... A foreign nationality, that is, a non-Soviet one, creates a hopeless muddle. You can't agree on anything.

MARTHA. I know Russian well. I studied it for five years. I've worked here almost three years. You understand me, don't you?

VOVA. I myself understand you, but you don't understand me. We've been standing here in the doorway for a solid hour, and we still don't know why you came here. There's some kind of American invasion happening here today.

MARTHA. Then she's here?

KIMBERLEY. I'm not trying to claim anything. I don't have any documents of ownership for this apartment. I just came to have a look. I heard so much at home about this place in my childhood that I even remembered the address, and so... My great-grandfather's alleyway really exists and the name hasn't changed, the building's still standing, it has all its floors and the apartment is intact. At home, when they used to talk about it it was like a fairy-tale, and now it suddenly exists, I reach out and touch it. I don't know how to explain it, but it's a miracle to me.

ILYA. You're a miracle yourself. Grandma, isn't she a delight?

ANASTASIA PETROVNA. Niusha, pass them their cereal, or else it will get cold.

Niusha crawls through the cage and passes them the cereal.

KIMBERLEY. Do we have to eat this?

ANASTASIA PETROVNA. If you're really from America, it's absolutely necessary. It's been a long trip, you must have gotten hungry.

NIUSHA (*touches the things on the chair*). Are these your things? Are they made in the USA?

KIMBERLEY. Mostly.

NIUSHA. Fantastic.

MARTHA (*in the hall*). I'm asking you, is Kimberley here?

VOVA. I don't know what you call her, but there's some girl who's latched on to Ilya again.

Knocks on the door.

ILYA. Pull the rope.

MARTHA knocks.

ILYA. (*in Russian*) Pull the rope, and the door will open.

MARTHA (*banging on the door and yelling*). Open up! Open up!

VOVA. What's your problem lady, don't you comprehend any language? He told you. Pull on the rope. (*He pulls*)

Martha runs into the room.

MARTHA. Kimberley!

KIMBERLEY. I'm here, you don't have to yell.

MARTHA. You didn't come home all night! I didn't know where to call, where to run! It's winter! There's snow, it's night!

ANASTASIA PETROVNA. Street, streetlight, drugstore.[1]

MARTHA. You call what you have in your city streetlights? They only illuminate the lamp-post! It's a good thing I remember your great-grandfather's former address. I've been rushing around since morning! And I don't have four-wheel drive. I skidded three times!

VOVA. You didn't forget to douse yourself with perfume.

MARTHA. Get up this minute. I'm taking you to the Kremlin and the Armory Palace today. And then to the theater this evening. What am I going to look like with you?

VOVA. That's the way to deal with her! Only you should have brought her up better, not now when she doesn't come home for the night.

NIUSHA (*in Russian*). She's not scolding, but inviting her to the Kremlin and the theater.

VOVA. To the Kremlin in this freezing weather? That's a severe form of punishment.

KIMBERLEY. To the Kremlin in this freezing weather? I've already seen the Kremlin.

MARTHA. Not only the Kremlin, but the Palace of Facets. It's heated.

KIMBERLEY. This apartment is heated, too, but you don't dare stick your head out from under the covers.

MARTHA. Listen, why is this absurd thing standing here? I can't get by.

ANASTASIA PETROVNA. Yes, really. Where did this delightful thing come from?

VOVA. I made it.

ANASTASIA PETROVNA. The grille-work is practically *art moderne*.

VOVA. I took the design from our bannister. But the grille-work is nothing. It's the internal construction that's the main thing. (*Gets into the cage*).

ILYA. This is the bliss of solitude.

KIMBERLEY. Why did he crawl inside the cage?

ILYA. Don't pay any attention to him. You and I were talking about something more interesting.

KIMBERLEY. About what?

ILYA. About morning kisses. And kisses come in the summer, winter, autumn, and spring varieties. (*Kisses her*).

KIMBERLEY. A morning kiss. It has a very special taste.

ILYA. What's it like?

KIMBERLEY. I haven't had a sufficient sampling.

Ilya prepares to kiss Kim again, but he's interrupted.

---

[1]From a poem by Aleksandr Blok

72

MARTHA. Kim, get up. We've got to get going.

ANASTASIA PETROVNA. Ilya, let the girl go, you see, they're expecting her.

ILYA. But I don't want to let her go.

KIMBERLEY. And I don't want to leave.

VOVA. (*from the cage*). Satan has a more pleasing form than Prince Charming himself.

MARTHA. Kim! I'm not just fooling around here! (*crawls through the cage*).

VOVA. (*in the cage*). American lady, not so rough!

MARTHA (in Russian). My name is Martha.

VOVA. Martha, Marfa, Well, at least your name is human.

MARTHA (*goes over to the ottoman*). I'm responsible to your parents for you. This is a foreign country, and it's not foreign like Italy, but really foreign. It's a whole other world You don't understand this yet. And these are foreign people. This young man… what have you found out about him that's worth lying under a blanket together?

KIMBERLEY. I know that his name is Ilya. He's a Russian. He's twenty like me. And he speaks English. You said they're a foreign people, but they all speak English here.

ANASTASIA PETROVNA. Of course we do. We speak it all the time when you aren't here.

NIUSHA. Anastasia Petrovna taught us.

ILYA. That's grandma.

ANASTASIA PETROVNA. And I was taught in my time by my grandmother. She taught me on purpose, because it was a useless thing to do.

MARTHA. English—useless?

ANASTASIA PETROVNA. The language of Shakespeare? In Moscow? Of course. We'll never see England or America, and here Niusha and I use it primarily in the kitchen.

KIMBERLEY. Why won't you see America? Ilya can come visit me. Will you come?

ILYA. To the USA? Would they really allow it?

VOVA. What can they have said that has Ilya dumbfounded?

NIUSHA (*in Russian*). She invited him to visit her in the USA.

VOVA. Oh, come on, off with you to the States. You think you found yourself an idiot? You think an honest man can get permission?

ANASTASIA PETROVNA. Yes, child, who do you think is going to let us go off to America?

KIMBERLEY. Martha, is this true? They have some kind of law that you can't visit friends in another country? Even if I invite him?

ANASTASIA PETROVNA. There's no such law. It's just not permitted.

MARTHA. No, as far as I know, immediate relatives are allowed to visit.

NIUSHA. What does "immediate relatives" mean?

MARTHA. Mothers, fathers, children, husbands and wives, brothers and sisters.

KIMBERLEY. That means if you're my husband, they'll let you come stay with me?

ILYA. Close one eye. Now make a wish.

KIMBERLEY. (*with one eye closed*) Now what?

ILYA. The one-eyed woman is daydreaming.

NIUSHA laughs.

KIMBERLEY. I don't understand. We talked all night... said so many things... about how great it will be to travel, see Europe together. I've hardly been anywhere, except with my parents... You don't want to marry me?

ILYA. Marry you?

KIMBERLEY. Aren't you listening?

ILYA. I'm listening, but sometimes I can't grasp the meaning.

KIMBERLEY. Why don't you ask?

ILYA. Well, it really doesn't matter to me what you say, I often can't make the words out. I just like to listen to you, just lie here and listen, I could lie here and listen to you endlessly.

KIMBERLEY. Listen? Listen to what?

ILYA. . It doesn't matter. If I'm not kissing your lips, at least I can watch them. All my life.

VOVA. What a language. Can't make out a single word.

NIUSHA (*speaking in Russian*). First she said that this is her great-grandfather's apartment, and then she understood that she can't move in here, because the law won't allow it, so she decided to have Ilya marry her.

VOVA. Here's what I say. Raggedy Andy the Higgledy-Piggledy sailed away on the raft with his little sidekick Sammie; he sailed to the Kam-River, from the Kam-River to the Tross-River, from the Tross-River to the Kubensk lake, from the Kubensk Lake to the Rostov Lake, and on that lake he asked to stay one night. One night grew to two nights, two night to two weeks, two weeks to two month, two months to two years, after two years he lived for thirty years.

KIMBERLEY. What was he going on so long about?

ILYA. . He said that you'll stay here to live. For thirty years.

KIMBERLEY. With you?

ILYA. With me.

KIMBERLEY. Then I agree. But everything sounds so long in Russian, it sounded as if he ennumerated each year individually.

ILYA. Do you want me to give you one kiss in advance for each year of our future life? (*He tries to kiss her*).

ANASTASIA PETROVNA. Ilya, you're not alone.

ILYA. (*stops kissing*). I know. Who would I kiss if I were alone? Only my dreams.

MARTHA. I don't understand anything. I suggest, Kim, that you get up quickly and get out of this apartment.

ILYA. And I understand everything, and I suggest to you, Kim, that you stay in this bed forever.

NIUSHA starts to crawl through the cage.

VOVA. Niusha, what are you doing? Were are you going? Have they said something to offend you? The devil brought them.

ANASTASIA PETROVNA. (*in Russian*). Well, yes, just try to explain how in our day and age two Americans suddenly appeared in this apartment.

ILYA. Vova! Grandma! What do you mean? (*in Russian*). Stop it! Stop.

VOVA. You stop yourself. Where from have they managed to descend on us?

ILYA. From America, of course, from many thousands of miles away, from America itself, and you... you didn't even offer them tea!

KIMBERLEY. No need for tea, it's time to get up.

ILYA. Get up? Why? You agreed to stay here for thirty years.

KIMBERLEY. But I don't have a visa for thirty years.

MARTHA. You don't even have one for thirty days. Don't forget that you have a fixed-date ticket. And you leave tomorrow morning.

ILYA. What do you mean, tomorrow morning?

ANASTASIA PETROVNA. Praise the lord.

NIUSHA (*drops back through the cage, to Vova*). They want to leave.

VOVA. That's bad form. You should offer guests a drink, at least a wee drop.

ILYA. Grandma! I know you've got some smoked sausage hidden away. Bring it as an appetizer.

ANASTASIA PETROVNA. But what's the cause for celebration, Ilya? You know how hard it was to get this sausage. I gave two years of my life for it. Maybe there won't be anymore sausage in my lifetime. If I put it away, it's not for myself, but for all of you, to eat at my wake.

ILYA. Not a wake, no, there's another word you taught us, Grandma. What is it?... Niusha, give me a hint...

NIUSHA. Funeral?

ILYA. What funeral, you idiot! I remember! Betrothal! This is our betrothal, isn't it? Isn't that the right English word?

KIMBERLEY. Yes, but we don't have betrothals anymore.

ILYA. You and I do.

MARTHA. And that's just fine. Let there be a betrothal. You'll leave me an invitation for your young man in which you'll write that he's your fiance. Get dressed, Kim.

KIMBERLEY. And if they won't let him out as my fiance?

MARTHA. They will, they will, just get dressed. And if they don't, he'll write you and you'll come here again. Just get dressed.

ANASTASIA PETROVNA exits.

NIUSHA (*Gives Kim her things*). Oh, how delightful! And how good they smell! Is this wool? But its as soft as silk. And don't you wear any underwear? Of course, it's warmer in America, you can go around in lace, but you can't get away without warm long pants here.

KIM gets dressed.

ILYA. I'll come to you, very soon, and we'll set out travelling.

KIMBERLEY. Let's make it during summer vacation?

ILYA. Fine. We'll travel to Italy for vacation, just as we planned.

KIMBERLEY. First we'll go to Rome by plane, then take a train to Florence, and go from there to Venice. From Florence to Venice is only about six or eight hours, I think.

ILYA. Are people really allowed to travel to Venice?

KIMBERLEY. Of course they are.

NIUSHA. You mean they let just anybody?

VOVA. Why does he have such a strange expression on his face? Is he really planning to go somewhere?

NIUSHA (*In Russian*). To Venice.

ILYA. Niusha, pass me the shot-glasses.

VOVA. They'll straighten him out in Venice.

ILYA. (*pours the vodka, speaking English and Russian*). Let's drink. Let's drink to my fate, to my love, to my happiness, to Kim! Where's Grandma?

ANASTASIA PETROVNA. (*entering with a plate of sausage*). Here. We're happy to have guests, never mind at what cost.

ILYA. Grandma, may you live eternally! You'll come visit us in America and speak English with the common people.

ANASTASIA PETROVNA. Now that I'll never do! Where do you get such banal ideas, Ilya? I didn't teach you English for you to get any practical use of it. It's true that there may be some decent people living in America, but judging how easy the living is there, they're all petty bourgeois, very bourgeois. What contemporary American is willing to put the impractical above the practical?

KIMBERLEY. I'm willing!

ILYA. Hoorah! To Kim!

NIUSHA. My God, smoked sausage! Just smell it, Martha, what an aroma!

KIMBERLEY. I've finished my drink. Now may I get washed up? And you get up too, Ilya. At least see me to my car.

ILYA. I'll see you to the car. But about getting washed up… That's a little more complicated. They shut off the hot water on Tuesday. And the cold… Grandma, at what time do they shut off the cold water today?

ANASTASIA PETROVNA. At nine o'clock.

ILYA. And what time is it now?

MARTHA. What a horror! It's almost eleven!

ILYA. That means it's too late for you to wash. Now it's only in the evening.

MARTHA. You'll wash at my place. Our water has been flowing continuously for a month, knock on wood.

KIM gets up ILYA sits on the ottoman.

KIMBERLEY. We won't be separated long. Only until summer. We'll write each other very, very, often. And then you'll come. We only have to wait for five months. Only five months and five days.

ANASTASIA PETROVNA. It seems to me the girl isn't dressed very warmly. We'll have to put a scarf on her.

MARTHA. I have a car waiting outside.

ANASTASIA PETROVNA. Your car may get stuck three times on the way. She can't go out without a scarf.

MARTHA. Kim, let's go.

KIMBERLEY. Ilya, why are you sitting down again? See me out.

ILYA. Why again? I was lying down before, and now I'm sitting. And don't rush me. You said "five months" and I suddenly pictured my room without you, and now my heart is breaking. How did I live before? Don't go, Kim. Stay here.

KIMBERLEY. But my visa.

ILYA. We'll hide you. No one will find out.

ANASTASIA PETROVNA. Ilya, don't be childish. (*In Russian*) Vova, help the ladies get out of here and give Kim my scarf from the coat-rack.

VOVA helps MARTHA and KIM crawl through the cage.

ILYA. *(stands up)*. Kim! Kim!

MARTHA and KIM, accompanied by VOVA, exit. ILYA collapses onto the ottoman. In the hall, VOVA puts a large scarf around Kim's neck and ties it. ILYA lies on the ottoman. On the edge of the ottoman sits his grandmother, NIUSHA is sitting on a chair nearby.

ANASTASIA PETROVNA. Don't cry, don't be sad, something will work out. It just doesn't happen that nothing works out.

ILYA. But she's not here anymore, Kim's not here.

ANASTASIA PETROVNA. It's all a dream, a dream, a delusion.

ILYA. Is a foreign country a dream?

ANASTASIA PETROVNA. Anything from abroad is a dream three times over.

NIUSHA. You must spit and say, whither night, thither dream. And then it's over.

ANASTASIA PETROVNA. In olden times people used to say prayers for those going to sleep.

NIUSHA *(corrects her) Before* going to sleep.

ANASTASIA PETROVNA. No, for those going to sleep, for those who come to you in your sleep.

ILYA. No, indeed! For the sleep of those coming into it. We ourselves go off into dream-land. And muddy its waters. And as soon as we come out if it, the dream flows by slowly and clearly.

NIUSHA. What's dreaming to some is waking to others. What's dreaming to some is reality to others.

ILYA. It's not dreaming, it wasn't a dream! The scent of her hair is still on the pillow.

VOVA *(enters, teasing)*. Reverend father, I want to marry! Mother, I want to marry!—So marry, my child!

ILYA. Grandmother! Why is he like that, why?... How can I go on without her?

ANASTASIA PETROVNA. What can you do! They say you can't spend your life in a lover's embrace.

ILYA. After her, go after her!

ANASTASIA PETROVNA. Where should we go, my child. It's all a myth, that America of yours, the fruits of some sick mind.

Day after day goes by, hour after hour, and soon five years, five months, and five days have passed without a trace. Ilya's room has not changed. Only the cage has been lifted from the floor and hung in the very middle of the high ceiling. Where most decent people have a candelabra, there is hanging a cage of unbelievable proportions, and inside it, a lamp-bulb has been let in like a bird. ILYA sits on his ottoman and looking at a glass mug which has a heating coil in it. He is waiting for the water to boil. He looks completely calm, demonstrates no bustling impatience; but then what is there to worry about,—electricity is a dependable thing, it won't deceive you, since water is supposed to boil, according to the mysterious laws of physics, that means, it will come to a boil. And when it comes to a boil, it will be possible to drink tea, and once having drunk tea, to decide what else to do. But there's no reason to react to the sharp ring at the door. Moreover, Vova is already

*shuffling out of his rooms along the corridor in his slippers. Vova opens the
door. And at the door is KIMBERLEY.*

VOVA. Wonder of wonders, miracle of miracles!...
KIMBERLEY. I'll say! (*goes to the door leading to Ilya's room, knocks.*)
ILYA. Pull the rope and the door will open.

KIM pulls the rope, the door opens, she enters.

ILYA. Kim, Kímushka! "I wandered lonely as a cloud..." What a vision! Is it
   really you?
KIMBERLEY. It's me, Ilya, it really is! Didn't you expect me?
ILYA. What do you mean, expect you, that's all I've been doing for five years, five
   months, and five days. You see the fringed tablecloth lies on the table awaiting
   your arrival. So that we can immediately set the table and give you tea after your
   journey. The last time we didn't get a chance to drink tea together.
KIMBERLEY. There's a lot we didn't manage to do last time. And what a lovely
   tablecloth it is.
ILYA. Here we call it our gem. My great-grandmother embroidered it with silk for
   the first male who would be born in her family. That means for me. So that my
   wife, looking at the tablecloth, would become kind and merry. Sit down and have
   some tea.
KIMBERLEY. Tea? In this heat?
ILYA. Then maybe you'd prefer vodka?
KIMBERLEY. No, no. Better have tea then.

ILYA, without getting up, brews tea and hands it to KIM.

ILYA. I have some *sushki*[1] to go with the tea. I bet you don't have *sushki* in
   America.
KIMBERLEY. We don't have *sushki*, but we do have sausage. Shall I get it out?
ILYA. Sausage? You want some sausage? Get it out of the refrigerator, you're
   closer. Niusha bought some this morning.
KIMBERLEY. But last time there wasn't any sausage in the stores. I brought you
   some from America.
ILYA. You should have brought a hunk of cheese, so at least we could remember
   what it smelled like. There isn't any cheese for sale anywhere. On the other hand,
   this is all nonsense. Though it's hardest of all to remember odors. I kept
   remembering your voice all the time..., but the scent of you... Sit down beside
   me, so that I can breathe in the aroma of you.

*KIM sits by ILYA on the ottoman, he embraces her, wants to kiss her. VOVA
enters.*

VOVA. In the old days, in olden times, after a mild spring, torrid summers would
   plague the earth. Mosquitoes and midges would appear, they would bite people
   and spill their hot blood.
ILYA. (*in Russian*). Vova! Why did you come in without knocking?

---

[1]small, donut-shaped pretzel

VOVA. Who made the hole in your door? I did. Who tied the rope? And it's my rope, by the way. I have the right to enter.

KIMBERLEY. What's he saying?

ILYA. He's saying that there are a lot of mosquitoes this summer and that the rope on the door is his.

KIMBERLEY. Well, let him untie it, take it, and leave.

ILYA. Then every second we'll have to get up to open the door.

KIMBERLEY. Ilya, Ilya, you're just the same, it's as if the past five years didn't exist.

ILYA. Since you're here, it means they didn't. (*Embraces her, tries to kiss her*).

VOVA. I can't see what there is to hug here. A strip of a girl, all elbows and knees.

KIMBERLEY. Why didn't you come? Why didn't you answer my letters?

ILYA. Man is his own worst enemy.

KIMBERLEY. Didn't you want to?

ILYA. Of course I wanted to. I wanted to very much. Oh, can it be possible to explain our life in English!

KIMBERLEY. All right, I won't ask. But now I know changes are occuring here. Things that weren't permitted have become possible. Let's get up right now and go. It's summer there, it's possible to go wherever one's fancy leads. And here is my great-grandfather's apartment, your great-grandmother's tablecloth. Do you understand me?

ILYA. God forbid! To look at you and on top of that to understand—that's more than a Russian can handle.

KIMBERLEY. Ach, Ilya, I'm serious. I have a job, a good job, and an apartment. Let's go.

ILYA. Is it possible in all of America you couldn't find anybody better?

KIMBERLEY. Nobody. Nobody but you exists for me on earth. I can't even imagine another husband for myself.

ILYA. But I don't even look like an American. Here that doesn't particularly matter, here everybody is a bit unusual. But in America, surrounded by Americans, you'll be ashamed that everybody else married a man and you married a gopher.

KIMBERLEY. You don't look like a gopher.

ILYA. Well, then, some other kind of animal, if not a beast.

KIMBERLEY. There's a fairy-tale called "Beauty and the Beast." She loves him and he turns into a human.

ILYA. It's you who have fairytales like that. We, on the other hand, have ones where you burn your wife's frog skin and instead of turning from a frog into a princess forever, she flies out an open window—and just try to catch her.

KIMBERLEY. That's true. That's a threat to her personal freedom. But I won't try to burn your Russian frog-prince skin.

ILYA. That's what you say now.

KIMBERLEY. Ilya! Ilya! Have you forgotten how it was in the winter, there was so much snow, and you gave it all to me as a present. And your grandmother gave me a scarf—see, I've brought it back with me.

ILYA. A scarf? I don't remember. But our climate really is horrible. Freezing in winter, sweltering in summer, rain in the fall.

KIMBERLEY. Did I come here for nothing?

ILYA. What do you mean! It's wonderful that you've come, it's a miracle that you're here—so cool in such heat. (*He embraces her, tries to kiss her*).

VOVA. It's the country-hopper! Just can't stay at home.

KIMBERLEY. What does he want now?

ILYA. He says that Americans travel a lot. And people who travel a lot must not be happy at home.

KIMBERLEY. You mean he thinks things are bad in America?

VOVA. Of course, we've never been in America, but I think it's no bowl of cherries. But there are worse countries. The English, for example , have traveled the world over, they discovered almost all the major rivers and mountains, that must mean that life at home is unbearable. And where can they find to live there in England? It's an island! What must it be like to know that your land isn't boundless?

KIMBERLEY. He's saying something bad about America.

ILYA. No, about England.

KIMBERLEY. Then let him.

ILYA. You've been away such a long time, Kim.

KIMBERLEY. You have a birthmark on your belly, down low. When I think about it, it makes me want to cry. Why is that so? A birthmark doesn't really tell you anything about a person, but I just can't bear remembering that little bit of you. It makes my heart ache.

ILYA. My little dove, how finely you've come to speak and feel...

KIMBERLEY. How?

ILYA. As if you were Russian. (*He embraces her, tries to kiss her*).

KIMBERLEY. Tell that Vova to go make another cage. For a birch-tree.

ILYA. He's an artist. He won't make the same thing twice.

KIMBERLEY. Then let him go make something else.

ILYA. He did. He made a little wagon that moves by itself, it starts up at the sound of a special whistle. I put my matchbox on this wagon—I'm always losing my matches, and now all you have to do is whistle and they come to you themselves. But then I lost the whistle. Vova got upset and now he makes nothing at all.

KIMBERLEY. Where is everybody else? Why doesn't anyone else pull the rope?

ILYA. Somebody will, just wait. It's very hot.

KIMBERLEY. And where are your parents?

ILYA. My parents? They're at our dacha. We have a wonderful dacha, Kim. We'll go there, you and I. There's woods and a stream. The stream's rather shallow, it's true, but so lively, winding, and very clear. You can see not only the rocks, but also sand on the bottom. In one spot the cows come to water, there, of course, the bank is mashed down, but it's on the other side. And on our side there is a gentle slope between old white willows; the sand there is soft, like your cheek. You can sit there, stretch your legs out against the water's flow, and listen to the water burble, rushing over your knees. And if you like to swim, a litttle farther down there's a, I don't know what it's called in English, suddenly there's this dark, deep, place. You understand?

KIMBERLEY. We'll go swimming there? Just the two of us?

ILYA. No, we can't go swimming together; I can't swim. I'll watch you.

Knock at the door.

ILYA. Pull on the rope and the door will open.

80

ANASTASIA PETROVNA. (*entering*). They've turned on the water. Whoever wants to take a shower, be my guest.

KIMBERLEY. Hello.

ANASTASIA PETROVNA. Hello, there. What has brought you here?

KIMBERLEY. Look, I've brought your scarf back.

ANASTASIA PETROVNA. No reason to worry. Such a fuss over a scarf.

KIMBERLEY. What fuss?

ANASTASIA PETROVNA. I don't know where you find to rush about to hither and thither in your America, but our house is hardly on your way.

KIMBERLEY. I'd like to take a shower, if I may.

ANASTASIA PETROVNA. You? I'm not so sure.

ILYA. The thing is that they've only turned on the cold water, the hot water is usually off completely for the summer.

ANASTASIA PETROVNA. And then our bathtub is missing one foot. During the war they dropped a bomb on the place, and it broke the foot off the bathtub. To stand up in our bathtub requires a long training period. (*in Russian*). Vova, they've turned on the water.

VOVA. Why didn't you say something? I haven't been able to catch the water since last week.

KIMBERLEY. (*pointing at the wall*). What's that? Over there?

VOVA. (*looking where she points*). Spidey.

ILYA. A spider.

KIMBERLEY. That big?

VOVA. We have wood-lice in the bathroom, and as for mice...

ILYA. He says that we have a lot of mice, and in the bathroom, I don't know what it's called in English, these many legged soft things crawl around.

VOVA. Creepy-crawlers.

ILYA. (*In Russian*). Bring some water.

VOVA takes a large pitcher in which there is a fine, cold ringing of silver spoons, and goes out.

ANASTASIA PETROVNA. God will not let the years pass by us, he won't. And spiders gather when there's news.

ILYA. Here's the news—Kim's come back.

ANASTASIA PETROVNA. So I see. You put out the family table-cloth.

KIMBERLEY. Martha brought me here. She'll come by for me soon.

ILYA. What for? Can't you stay?

KIMBERLEY. Martha doesn't think so. My parents said five years ago that it wouldn't work out for you and me, because you're Russian and I'm American.

ILYA. Niusha's parents said the same thing, and everything worked out for Niusha and me. Vanka's going to be two soon. And it'll work out with you, too.

KIMBERLEY. Who's Vanka?

ANASTASIA PETROVNA. My great-grandson, Ivan Ilich, that means the son of my grandson Ilya.

ILYA. You see, we hung the cage up for him. He sat there, and didn't bother anybody and wasn't bored himself—observed life from above. And now he's walking already, so we had to put the light-bulb in the cage.

Piercing screams and moans are heard.

KIMBERLEY. What's that?

ILYA. That's Vova in the bathtub—the water is ice-cold. I don't know where they get it from.

ANASTASIA PETROVNA. I like the water that way—it's scary and light, and painful.

KIMBERLEY. You seem to be speaking in verse all the time.

ANASTASIA PETROVNA. Of course I speak in verse. In my own English translation.

Ring at the door.

And you, Kim, do you like poetry?

The ring is repeated.

KIMBERLEY. Poetry? I don't know. That's probably Martha.

ANASTASIA PETROVNA. Can you recite us something contemporary? I haven't read any new poetry in a long time.

The ring is repeated.

KIMBERLEY. Somebody should open it.

ILYA. Vova will open it.

KIMBERLEY. But he's in the bathroom. Taking a shower.

ILYA. He'll finish up and open the door. What's the rush?

The ring is repeated. Along the corridor, carrying a quieted pitcher of water, moves Volodya, He opens the door. At the door is Martha.

MARTHA. I thought everyone in here had died.

VOVA. And we wish you the same,

MARTHA. Hello.

VOVA. You are like a wind from fields of clover.

MARTHA. Do you like my new perfume?

VOVA. This type of conversation won't get anywhere with me.

MARTHA. What conversation?

VOVA. The kind that goes. You've touched my arm, so you've got to marry me— look here—I've a bald patch that shines, and my maiden name still on my passport. We have a saying—marry, and you take out a century-long mortgage on your life! And a century can last a long time.

MARTHA. The Russian language really is difficult. I didn't understand a thing you said. Try to speak slower.

VOVA. Slower, it sounds like this: you've got no business here, excuse my rudeness. They can't live a minute without each other, that's how well suited they are to each other.

MARTHA. Who?

VOVA. You-know-who. Whether we love her or not, we'll hold her hand.

MARTHA. No, it's much easier to live when you don't know any foreign languages. Especially Russian.

KIMBERLEY. *(in the room).* I'm sure that's Martha. It's time for me to go.

ILYA. Why go? What for?

KIMBERLEY. Because you have everything already.

ILYA. What have I got? I don't understand.

KIMBERLEY. A family.

ILYA. The one doesn't have to interfere with the other. Don't complicate everything in your American way.

KIMBERLEY. What should I do?

ILYA. Don't do anything. It's so tiring to chose between forms, formlessness is so much nicer and calmer.

VOVA. (*in the hall*). And maybe you know German, too?

MARTHA. Both German and French. But for some reason I understand more when I'm in those countries.

VOVA. Somehow I can't figure out the difference between those nations. They're all clean, smell of cologne, and spend their time doing business. I even feel sorry for you all. I look at your America and your Europe on television, like a bachelor looks at the home of his future mother-in-law. It's clean, but seems full of horrors.

MARTHA. Without your eloquence and your bombs, nobody would know of the existence of Russians on earth.

VOVA. You don't like us?

MARTHA. It's not that I don't like you, it's that I get mad all the time. It's not possible to deal with you calmly. Everything inside (*puts her hand to her chest*) starts to boil up.

VOVA. Would you like some cold water?

MARTHA. I don't drink your water.

VOVA. Then why do you live here?

MARTHA. The water in America is better...

VOVA. American water.

MARTHA. In America I don't get mad at anyone.

VOVA. There aren't many Russians there.

MARTHA. In America I'm calm. Do you understand? No feelings. Absolute peace and calm. Like in a grave.

VOVA. I understand. Let's go ask Ilya for some vodka. We'll get it ice-cold out of his freezer and drink it not in gulps but in kisses.

MARTHA comes to the door, knocks.

ILYA. Pull it, pull it!

MARTHA pulls the rope and enters.

KIMBERLEY. Martha! (*Rushes towards her and weeps bitterly*).

MARTHA. I told you that you shouldn't come here alone.

ILYA. Why shouldn't she? Let us sort things out for ourselves. Kim, don't cry, please don't cry. I can't stand to see your tears.

MARTHA. You've tortured her!

ILYA. What do you mean, Martha! Look at me—I've been tortured to death myself.

MARTHA. I know, I know, first you torture yourself over one woman, then you get married to another.

VOVA. (*enters with a pitcher*). How can one exchange one's own kind, a Russian woman, for some American or other.

ILYA. But she's a woman, too.

VOVA. Nonsense! What kind of woman is she? It's only in appearance, but there's no womanly content in her and there can't be any.

ANASTASIA PETROVNA. Don't cry, Kim. A new love will grow soon. But you must water it not with tears, but with blood.

KIM (*draws back*). Crazy! You're all crazy!

ANASTASIA PETROVNA. It's only Russian poetry in my free English translation.

Niusha runs in.

NIUSHA. Cheese! Cheese is back!

ANASTASIA PETROVNA. (*in Russian*). My God! Where?

VOVA. Yes, where?

NIUSHA. In the store on the corner!

KIMBERLEY. What happened?

MARTHA. They're saying that somebody's come back, probably some relative.

NIUSHA. Here! (*gets a hunk of cheese out of her bag and puts it on the table*).

ILYA. It really is cheese. How long has it been since we've seen each other? A year? Or more? Kim, sit down to the table. Everyone sit down. We'll have a festival in honor of the return of cheese. Let's get the vodka out of the freezer.

Everyone takes a place around the table, they get out the vodka and shot-glasses, cut the cheese.

NIUSHA. Did you get out this table cloth in honor of the cheese?

ILYA. No in Kim's honor. Kim! Kim, where are you?

Kim and Martha have left the room.

Year after year passes, like water passing throuogh your fingers. A full palm, and five fingers, like five years; you look and don't remember what happened to you during those five years, how the time was filled.

There was Moscow—an ancient city, and though its alleyways are dilapidated, it still stands to this day. Neither the country, nor the government stands, but Moscow—is still here. Life occurs not in a government, but in a home. Only our home is undergoing changes, as if a black whirlwind had blown in: the authorities decided that the people were hindering the process of repairs, so they're moving everybody out. Tie up your bundles, pull the drawstrings of your knapsacks, gather your spoons and your saucers—they're driving you to a foreign land. Time is behind us, time is before us, but not with us. The door to the apartment is wide-open—they're leaving, what is there for us here... Kim enters—there's no one, knocks on Ilya's door. Silence. She knocks again. No answer. Then she pulls on the rope and the door opens. In Ilya's room something has changed, although only one cabinet has been moved. Oh, there it is, behind the cabinet is revealed a tall white set of folding doors. And there is no more cage hanging from the ceiling. Neither is there a light-bulb—lightbulbs have disappeared from the country. Kim doesn't know about this and didn't bring any light-bulbs—but that would have made an excellent present. Instead she must look into the half-darkness of the room, which unites and makes live creatures kin to dead objects.

KIMBERLEY. (*pausing*). Is there anybody here?

There is motion on the ottoman.

ILYA. There is. Pull the rope.
KIMBERLEY. I already pulled it and entered.
ILYA. Then turn on some lamp, whichever one works.

Kim turns on a table-lamp.

ILYA. What happened? Why in the middle of the night?
KIMBERLEY. It's day-time now. It's only five o'clock.
ILYA. Then why is it dark?
KIMBERLEY. Because it's dark outside. And it's dark outside because they haven't turned on the street-lights yet.
ILYA. For some reason whenever I look out the window, I can't see anything but night. I used to be able to see roof-tops, a lot of different rooftops. And above one house there were always birds flying around. Above others there were none, but over this particular one they just kept circling and circling. And that made it very alarming. Now they're showing us darkness. And calling it—day. How long was I asleep?
KIMBERLEY. And you would have slept even longer, if I hadn't come.
ILYA. If you hadn't come. And who are you. I can't see you behind the lamp.
KIMBERLEY. You weren't expecting me?
ILYA. Come here. Kim? Kimmie! I was waiting for you, I was waiting!
KIMBERLEY. You were sleeping.
ILYA. I was sleeping so that the time would pass more quickly. How prompt you are!
KIMBERLEY. Why prompt? What day is it?
ILYA. Thursday. My day is Thursday. My color is blue. My gem-stone is a diamond.
KIMBERLEY. Ilya, I called you. You were going to come to meet me.
ILYA. You called. I remember. Of course you called. We spoke on the phone. I could hear you as well as if you were near, only hiding, I wanted to reach out my arms, embrace you, and draw you to me. (*He embraces Kim*).
KIMBERLEY. Why didn't you meet me?
ILYA. I fell ill.
KIMBERLEY. Get up. You know I haven't got much time.
ILYA. How can I know?
KIMBERLEY. I told you on the phone (*points to the telephone*)—there's the telephone, you understand? —I said, that I was coming to Moscow on a business trip. And you, you asked me to meet with you. You said that you really needed to. What did you need?
ILYA. But you were the one who called?
KIMBERLEY. I did.
ILYA. And I was the one who needed something?

KIMBERLEY. Who can figure you out, maybe your telephone only works in one direction and I can call you, but you can't call out. That's why I called. What did you need?

ILYA. Some kind of medicine.

KIMBERLEY. What kind of medicine?

ILYA. To make it easier. You seem to have a medicine for everything in your country.

KIMBERLEY. There's none for this.

ILYA. Well, all right. It will go away. Especially since if we drink vodka in honor of your arrival, it will become easier.

KIMBERLEY. Get up.

ILYA. Wait a minute. Not everything right away. Let me look at you. You look wonderful. Wonderful… But you've become so… grown up. A real lady.

KIMBERLEY. I'm thirty years old. And I'm already a manager.

ILYA. You—a manager. Oh, I can't take it. You, Kim, a manager?

KIMBERLEY. Yes. And what about it?

ILYA. It's funny.

KIMBERLEY. But you look pretty bad. Very bad, even. But somehow you haven't changed. The same childlike face.

ILYA. And my birthmarks are still in place. Do you want to check them?

KIMBERLEY. No. Not just one year has passed, not just two, and you're still a little kid. That just can't be. It contradicts the laws of nature.

ILYA. Your laws, maybe. And then, what is a year. Years can be different. There are light-years, and astronomical years, there are years measured by the Julian calendar, by the Gregorian, which is whole hours shorter than the Julian, there are star years and moon years, and something called a Platonic year— it contains twenty-five normal years, I think,—that's my year. The years have been completely platonic and so long. (*He embraces her, tries to kiss her.*)

KIMBERLEY. You have such a young face!

ILYA. How can I count the years, since without you I didn't live.

KIMBERLEY. You didn't live? You have a son who's already going to school!

ILYA. To my Russian ear that sounds like a reproach. As a matter of fact, he just missed an entire year of school.

KIMBERLEY. Did something happen? He got sick?

ILYA. Quite the contrary. Judging by the photographs, he's grown up and gotten stronger. There's good food in Israel.

KIMBERLEY. He doesn't live with you any more?

ILYA. Do you mean to ask if I separated from Niusha? I did. More precisely, she separated from me.

KIMBERLEY. I mean to ask just what I ask. Or do you find that I speak English poorly?

ILYA. You speak it no worse than my grandmother, and nobody spoke better English in my presence than my grandmother.

KIMBERLEY. Her English is good, but a little archaic.

ILYA. But lovely. To you, maybe, even Shakespeare is archaic. You're always rushing ahead.

KIMBERLEY. Is Niusha really Jewish?

ILYA. What do you mean, what kind of Jew do you think she is? Now her parents really were Jewish. They left a long time ago and called her to come, but she stayed here with me.

KIMBERLEY. Did they get her out of an orphanage?

ILYA. Why an orphanage?

KIMBERLEY. Well, since they were Jews and she wasn't, that means she was adopted, doesn't it?

ILYA. How you... you really don't understand anything. She was their own daughter, and so much like her father, that you can't tell their baby pictures apart. Only Niusha wasn't Jewish at all.

KIMBERLEY. Niusha's a very Russian name.

ILYA. Niusha—a Russian name? It's from Anna!

KIMBERLEY. Then I don't understand. You married her, because she wasn't a Jew? Or because she was?

ILYA. I married her because I loved her. And whether she was a Jew, a Mordovian, or a Chuvash... You probably haven't even heard of those peoples?

KIMBERLEY. But she emigrated as a Jew.

ILYA. She did. Was a non-Jew, became a Jew —that could happen to anybody.

KIMBERLEY. It seems I don't understand English very well.

ILYA. A Jew is a person who thinks that he's not like everybody else here. You're American for the same reason. In our country most people don't have any nationality — all their grandmothers and grandfathers were of different bloods. We're Russian by language, but by blood—we're Soviet. And then they suddenly announce that it's impossible to live here anymore. Why not? Who measured the possible and impossible? And there's no sensible answer. She just up and left. And she took Vanka and the cage with her.

KIMBERLEY. What will she need such a large cage for in Israel?

ILYA. I don't know. To hold a singing Arab, probably.

KIMBERLEY. But why didn't you leave with her?

ILYA. I couldn't leave.

KIMBERLEY. Why not?

ILYA. What do you mean, why not? You might come, and I wouldn't be home. I tried to go outside as seldom as possible. I was waiting for you. (*He embraces her and finally kisses her.*)

The tall shutter-like doors are flung open with a knock. From then emerges Vova, proudly carrying two doll-house chairs. Behind him can be seen a suite of half-empty rooms, tall and sad in their state of ruin.

VOVA. A Russian soul is the soul of a woman! We cherish and treasure all kinds of junk.

KIMBERLEY. Hello, Vova.

VOVA. Foo, foo! Neither hide nor hair of our American, and suddenly she appears on our doorstep. And what a beauty she's become!

KIMBERLEY. If he takes such a long time just to greet me, you don't have to translate.

VOVA. Don't get too close to him, he's got the shakes.

ILYA. He thinks I have a fever.

KIMBERLEY. I'll give you some aspirin.

ILYA. That's not necessary. Let's drink some vodka instead. (*In Russian*). Vova, come sit down to the table with us.

VOVA. I don't have time. I have to carry out my things. We ordered a taxi. I don't know what you're thinking about, just a-sittin' there.

ILYA. (*In Russian*). But if not here, then were should we live? I can't imagine.

VOVA. Where, where, in the air—any empty place will do *(exits)*.

ILYA. (*pours the vodka*). Let's drink to your arrival. Now I won't gaze out on stranger's rooftops and count the ravens, I'll gaze on you. I'm ready to sit near you a very, very long time and just gaze and gaze.

KIMBERLEY. And not do anything?

ILYA. Nothing at all. Except maybe eat and drink. Just so you'll be next to me or, for variety, sit across from me.

KIMBERLEY. And won't you get sick of that?

ILYA. God, no.

KIMBERLEY. But you were sitting like this before.

ILYA. Not like this at all. How could it be like this if you weren't next to me? I've only sat like this twice in my life, and today is the third time—— now it's forever. I'm beginning a new life.

KIMBERLEY. One begins a new life with the new year, or on a Monday at least.

ILYA. And I begin with the letter "a". It's the first letter of all the European alphabets, except Runic. Why all except Runic, do you know?

KIMBERLEY. No.

ILYA. Neither do I. And now I won't even find out. In my new life I won't need senseless knowledge. I know "A" and that's enough. In Slavonic it's "az" -that means I have much sinned. In Greek "alpha" and in Phoenician "alef" or the bull. We'll roast him and eat him in honor of the prodigal wife Kimberley. How many words do you know that begin with the letter "a"?

KIMBERLEY. I never thought about it.

ILYA. Well. There are practically no words in Russian beginning with "a", if you don't count as Russian such delightful words as "ad"—in English that's"Hell" and "Ataman" or Cossack chieftan. Well, Kim, what about a non-Russian word beginning with the letter "a"?

KIMBERLEY. Adam.

ILYA. Adam? Wonderful. The first man. Az yesm' Adam. I am Adam, I am the first man. I am alone. There is no one else. Come here, Kim. (*Hugs her, attempts to kiss her*).

The door to the room opens without a knock, VOVA returns.

VOVA. Well, not in vain did you struggle and suffer. Search the whole world over, and you'll not find another such beauty as this Militrissa Kirbitievna.

ILYA. (*in Russian*). I propose we drink to that! (*In English*). He says there's no beauty in the world quite like you.

VOVA. Only you'll never really see her, just as you'll never see your own ears.

ILYA. (*drinks*). But I'll never see you, as I'll never see my own ears.

KIM (*drinks*). To the mirror!

ILYA. What mirror?

KIMBERLEY. In which you see your ears.

88

From the open doors in the suite of rooms emerges ANASTASIA PETROVNA with a toy hand-mirror in her hands.

ANASTASIA PETROVNA. This suite, I think, was specially designed for ease of moving things out.

ILYA. Grandma, come to us.

ANASTASIA PETROVNA. Greetings, Kim. You've come at just the right moment.

KIMBERLEY. Greetings. And I was thinking just the opposite. You're moving.

ANASTASIA PETROVNA. Yes, we're moving. Absolutely everyone is being moved out, but Ilya Ilich just lies there and won't budge.

ILYA. What do you mean, just lies there? I'm sitting up.

ANASTASIA PETROVNA. We need your help, Kim. Maybe you can get him out of here. I don't have the strength any more.

ILYA. Grandma, give me the mirror for a second (*he takes the toy hand-mirror*). My ears! I see my ears! Your Russian folk wisdom is mistaken, Vova.

VOVA. I'm not obliged to understand remarks from foreigners. (*he takes the toy mirror from Ilya and carries it out.*)

ILYA. Grandma! But what about you? Can you really be moving to a new apartment?

ANASTASIA PETROVNA. How boring, cold, and painful. (*She goes out into the back of the suite.*)

KIMBERLEY. Is that poetry?

ILYA. I hope so.

KIMBERLEY. I don't understand; everyone's moving, but you?...

ILYA. I'm staying here with you.

KIMBERLEY. But the repairs!

ILYA. There are always some repairs going on. And besides, maybe they won't even do the repairs, since it's cheaper just to demolish the building.

KIMBERLEY. But they'll turn off the water, the gas, the electricity, and the heat.

ILYA. They've already turned off the water, and they haven't turned the heat on yet this year, But let's drink some vodka, we'll get drunk and it will warm us up. As far as electricity is concerned... There's a Russian saying. You're the light of my eyes.

KIMBERLEY. You really are a child. You can't be left here alone. Here things really are bad, life is hard, everything is falling apart, and you don't have any work, it seems.

ILYA. It seems I don't. However, I can't remember.

KIMBERLEY. I'll take you away. That will be my personal humanitarian aid to Russia.

ILYA. Take me away. In a suitcase, if you like, in a basket, if you prefer. You'll take me as checked baggage. Only don't lose me or leave me alone. Never.

KIMBERLEY. I don't have much time. Together we won't manage to get everything done. All right, let's go now, I'll introduce you to a man who works in our embassy. He'll help you. First you'll come as a tourist, as my guest. I'll leave you money for a ticket, no, better I buy you the ticket myself. Why do you look like that? What are you thinking about?

ILYA. About you. How you walk, in a special way, as if you were on an invisible tightrope. How you wave your hands when you talk, I would like to kiss every finger of yours.

Vova enters.

(*In Russian*). Vova! I'm leaving. I'm going with Kim.

VOVA. Go, go. They live wealthily, they have a ringlike courtyard three poles end to end, with three stakes in it, three sticks wound around it, the sky for a roof and surrounded by light. You'll live happily and healthily, with your fists.

KIMBERLEY. Is that poetry again?

ILYA. It's worse. He thinks that you aren't so very rich and I'll be one more mouth to feed.

KIMBERLEY. You'll go to work. It's not clear yet which of us will make more in the long run.

ILYA. I'll go work?

ANASTASIA PETROVNA. (*at the end of the suite*). Vova!

KIMBERLEY. Won't you?

ILYA. No, I'm prepared, for your sake, I'm prepared for far more. But what work will I do?

KIMBERLEY. And what did you do here?

ILYA. I day-dreamed, fantasized. Do they have a job like that in America?

ANASTASIA PETROVNA. (*from the end of the suite*). Vova!

KIMBERLEY. She seems to be calling for Vova.

ANASTASIA PETROVNA enters.

VOVA. We'll be rolling along. What's to worry about? Let's have a final drink to the city of Moscow, to sadness and longing, to the sunrise and sunset, for life before payday, to swiftly-passing youth and pure tears.

ILYA. (*pours everyone vodka*). Let's drink, Kim, as Vova proposes, to swiftly-passing youth and pure tears.

KIMBERLEY. Why does it sound like poetry in Russian and prose in English? And why to tears? What should we cry for?

ANASTASIA PETROVNA. For everything that can't be helped.

KIMBERLEY. Poetry again?

ANASTASIA PETROVNA. Yes. (*In Russian*). Let's go, Vova, I'm afraid we'll lose our taxi.

ANASTASIA PETROVNA and VOVA go out into the end of the suite. ILYA lies down on the ottoman.

KIMBERLEY. You're down again? I just knew it.

ILYA. Of course you knew. I have the feeling that we have never, ever, parted. We've lived together all these years and we'll continue to live together and die on the same day.

KIMBERLEY. Where will we live, if your house is either being repaired or maybe completely demolished?

ILYA. At our dacha. Have I told you what a remarkable dacha we have? The landscape is completely Russian, that is, there's nothing remarkable about it, but everything's soft and gentle. My whole family will gather there. Mama and Papa, you and I, our children.

KIMBERLEY. So many people... What kind of house do you have?

ILYA. It's quite spacious. It's quiet.

KIMBERLEY. With so many people around—it's quiet?

ILYA. Yes, quiet. Grandma's like a mouse, goes shush-shush, Papa spends all day at the river fishing, and Mama doesn't stick her nose out of the kitchen, she boils and bakes, and calls us to table four times a day. I've been dreaming about going there for a long time, only I lacked a wife, that's why I appoint you.

KIMBERLEY. And just when do you plan to go there?

ILYA. Tomorrow, if you like. The weather should be marvelous. From our house to the station stretches a lane of lime-trees, and as you walk along it, you sense a gentle ringing above your head—it's the sound of bees collecting lime-tree honey. And the scent of it is so light and sweet. Right now the lime-trees are in bloom.

KIMBERLEY. Right now it's October.

ILYA. Oh, why must you say things like that?

KIMBERLEY. Why must I say things like that? No, why must you say things like that? Everything you said is a lie. And now I know it's a lie. Your father died a long time ago, and your mother remarried and has been living in America for a number of years. You are alone, alone with your half-witted grandmother. And you sold the dacha a long time ago, you have no dacha!

ANASTASIA PETROVNA and VOVA appear with the remains of the doll-house furniture in their hands.

ANASTASIA PETROVNA. We'll let's sit down in preparation for the journey, have a moment of silence.

All sit down, are silent, then stand up.

ANASTASIA PETROVNA. I, Iliusha, am an old woman, may God give me the strength to manage myself, but you, young people, I warn you that we're the last ones left in this building and they're turning off the electricity today, the elevator will stop and there'll be no light. And without an elevator I won't be able to crawl out of here. Here's a candle for you just in case. (*Puts a candle on the table.*). Farewell.

VOVA. Have a nice stay.

ANASTASIA PETROVNA and VOVA exit.

ILYA. Vova said, "Have a nice stay." So we're going to be happy here. Quick, crawl under the covers with me, now nobody else will come in.

The lights go out.

They really did turn it off. I hope they managed to get down by the elevator.

KIM lights the candle.

Well, come to me.

KIMBERLEY. No.

ILYA. Why?

KIMBERLEY. Because. I'm leaving.

ILYA. The elevator isn't working anymore.

KIMBERLEY. I can take the stairs.

ILYA. Where to?

KIMBERLEY. Wherever my feet will carry me. Just out of here.

ILYA. Don't, Kim. Stay here. For a year, for a day. It's in your best interests—you'll become young, too. Just a girl. As it was then, you remember. When you stayed here for the night.

KIMBERLEY. In my best interests! You, a Russian, are telling me this? That I am operating in my own interest here?

ILYA. Who the hell can figure out what your words mean; well, I used the wrong word, excuse me. You might have learned Russian yourself, in order to understand something about our life.

KIMBERLEY. I don't want to. I don't want to know anything, or try to understand. I want to go home, to America. And I'm leaving.

ILYA. But I won't let you go.

KIMBERLEY. You? Won't let me go? To do that you'd have to get up and hold the door shut?

ILYA. Why should I hold the door shut, the lock will hold it.

KIM turns and sees a large lock hanging on the door, goes up to it, pulls on it, the lock doesn't budge.

KIMBERLEY. Give me the key.

ILYA. There is no key.

KIMBERLEY. Give me the key.

ILYA. I'm telling you, there's no key to this lock.

KIMBERLEY. And I'm telling you for the last time—give me the key.

ILYA. I love you.

KIM takes a knife, goes up to ILYA and strikes him with the knife. She stands in amazement, then takes ILYA by the shoulder easily, turns him over and sits him up: out of an opening in his chest pour out rags, papers, sawdust, dry leaves, his rag-doll arms and legs hang lifelessly, a painted face smiles at her.

KIMBERLEY. Well, that's my humanitarian aid to Russia.

The lock hangs on the door.

THE END

BIOGRAPHIES

MARIA ARBATOVA (b. 1957) gained early literary success as a poet, published in the prestigious literary journals *Moskva* and *Novy mir*. At first attracted to the study of philosophy, she abandoned Moscow University in her second year to enroll in the Gorky Literary Institute. Several of her plays, notably *Viktoria Vasilieva As Seen by Outsiders, Alekseev and the Shadows*, and *On the Road to Ourselves* have been published by *Sovremennaia dramaturgiia*. To her successes as a poet and dramatist, Arbatova has added journalistic renown, with regular opinion pieces and interviews in the newspapers *Gumanitarnyi fond, Obshchaia gazeta*, and others. Her first short story, *Abortion from an Unbeloved*, won the newspaper's prize for best story of 1993. Since 1994, she has become a regular participant in television talk shows including the women's show *I, Myself* and several of her plays have been broadcast on radio in Germany. Arbatova's active political stance (she is president of a liberal feminist organization, "Harmony") is reflected in her recent plays, *An Experimental Interview on the Theme of Freedom*, and *The Taking of the Bastille. Equation with Two Knowns* is in rehearsal at the "Looking Glass" Theatre in New York City.

ELENA GREMINA (b. 1956) hails from a renowned family of cinematographers. A graduate of the Gorky Literary Institute, she had her first major production at the Leningrad Theater for Young Spectators, where her play *The Myth of Svetlana*, with music by the popular singer-songwriter Veronica Dolina in 1984 gained critical praise but official censorship. Her plays *The Wheel of Fortune* and *The Cornet O-va Affair* have been published in *Teatr*, the main organ of the Union of Theatrical workers. With her husband, playwright Mikhail Ugarov, she authored the popular television 1994 serial *Russian Secrets*. She is author of numerous plays for both stage and radio. *The Cornet O-va Affair* received critical acclaim in a 1993 production at the Omsk Dramatic Theater (Siberia) under the direction of Lev Stukalov, which was produced at the Komissarzhevskaia Theater in St. Petersburg in 1994. The Russian version of *Behind the Mirror* was published in *Dramaturg* in 1994. Gremina's radio-plays have aired widely in Germany and Russia. Recent works include *My Friend, Repeat after Me,* and *The Wife of Sakhalin.* Since 1995, Gremina, Ugarov, and Mikhailova have become the newest members of the "Areopagus" of dramatists and critics to select the works to be shown at the International Festival of Young Dramatists at Liubimovka, the former estate of Konstantin Stanislavsky.

OLGA MIKHAILOVA (b. 1953) began her intellectual development as a student of history at the Bibliographic-Archival Institute, where her professors warned her that her original thinking would bode no good in the world of Soviet professional historians. Playwrighting initially proved a more lucrative profession, and she became the author of numerous short plays and filmscripts, winning

93

recognition in 1987 with the production of *Holiday* /Praznichnyi den'/ at the Theater of the Lenin Komsomol in Moscow, under the direction of Vladimir Mirzoyev, (who directed *Russian Dream* in Canada in 1994). She has collaborated on several joint Russian-French film and theater productions. Her *The Bride-to-Be* and *The Archer* plays have been published in Russia in the journals *Siuzhety* and *Dramaturg*, respectively. Her radio play, *Deep Waters* won the prize as best radio play of 1992 and premiered on Moscow Radio in 1993. A recent play, *Giselle*, which studies the confrontation between an American Vietnam-era psychiatrist and recent Russian war veterans, is scheduled for production at Moscow's Mayakovsky Theater. Mikhailova has also written numerous plays for children, including *The Childhood of Robinson Crusoe*, produced in 1994 at Moscow's *Theater of the Moon*.

MELISSA T. SMITH (translator and editor) is an Associate Professor in the Department of Foreign Languages at Youngstown State University (Youngstown, Ohio, USA). She is the author of several articles on 20th century Russian women playwrights in the collections *Dictionary of Russian Women Writers*, *Russian Women Writers*, the journals *Slavic and East European Arts* and *Theater Three*. In addition to the works in this volume, she has translated plays by Liudmila Petrushevskaia and Liudmila Razumovskaia. She has also served as editor-in-chief of the volume *Ivan Elagin: In Memoriam* for *Canadian-American Slavic Studies*.

Other titles in the Russian Theatre Archive series: